BATHROOM

Remodeling with an Architect

Design Ideas to Modernize Your Bathroom

THE LATEST TRENDS +50

HOME PRESS

CONTENTS

INTRODUCTION

R eady for a bathroom renovation? In this delicate building intervention, it is in fact good to keep in mind that every modification we make will have the ability to affect the design, functionality and use of this important home environment.

In order to obtain the best results, therefore, also by optimizing costs, it is very important to keep in mind these 8 things to know in preparation for a flawless bathroom renovation.

CHOICE OF SANITARY WARE

In a bathroom renovation it is important to consider where the connection to the drainage sewer system is located as well as that relating to the water load (cold / hot drinking water).

Excluding specific cases, the goal should be to rethink our bathroom while keeping these systems as fixed points of our project. Avoiding the relocation of these pipelines would be an excellent way to shorten the timing of the works and the resulting economic expense. Here, thanks to this expedient, we could therefore allocate part of this to other restructuring aspects such as the choice of bathroom fixtures.

- Wc and bidet: on the market there are mainly two types available: wall-mounted and floor-mounted. The former has greater aesthetic impact, do not require silicone closures (yielding over time), but generally have higher costs and require sufficiently thick walls within which to place the drain pipes. The traditional floor-mounted sanitary ware, on the other hand, is cheaper, more practical (given their ability to connect the pipes both to the ground and to the wall) but certainly of lesser aesthetic impact. Regardless of the aspect to which you want to give more priority (aesthetic or practical), it is good to make this type of choice from the beginning of the bathroom renovation given their impact on the duration and type of plumbing intervention necessary.
- Washbasin: this sanitary ware also certainly occupies an important position in the bathroom of the house. There are mainly three types on the market to choose from: 1.

pedestal washbasin is generally the cheapest, even if hygienically less practical than other types; in fact, in the rear part of the structure the accumulation of dust and the lack of support space make it not very functional. 2.Wall-hung washbasin which is also generally inexpensive and thanks to its anchoring to the wall it is able to allow easier cleaning of the underlying flooring. If the variant with half-column is chosen, it is also possible to hide the pipes inside the structure itself.

Countertop washbasin certainly represents a modern and trendy choice with an impactful design capable of providing personality to our bathroom. Against this choice is that relating to the choice of taps. In fact, for this structure it is necessary to purchase, in most cases, high-barreled taps - generally more expensive as well.

BATH OR SHOWER?

If you really can't decide why not choose on the basis of the space available? Where the size of the room is reduced, the installation of the shower would certainly represent a more practical and dynamic option - as well as easier if you have elderly people in the family unit. If, on the other hand, the size of the room allows it, installing a standard bathtub or a combined solution (bathtub with shower function) could also represent a valid alternative.

Regardless of your choice, it is very important to make sure that the installation of the chosen sanitary ware does not represent an obstacle to movement within the room itself.

THE EYE PLAYS ITS PART

Let's face it: a room like the bathroom must certainly satisfy our practical needs, without neglecting our ego. The advice for an excellent bathroom renovation is therefore to allocate part of our budget to furniture, mirrors and lights. These three aspects, if jointly harmonized, are really able to provide a significant improvement contribution. And if the eye really plays its part, the painting of the bathroom walls can certainly not be overlooked, because of its great impact at a small price. Specifically, the use of light-colored breathable paints could really give this part of the house a real relaxing atmosphere.

TRANSPIRATION OF ENVIRONMENTS

Does your bathroom already have escape routes to vent water vapor and stale air? A window (or the installation of a controlled ventilation system in the absence of windows) is an essential bathroom renovation operation to allow proper ventilation of the room. In this context it would be really good to apply a breathable paint to the walls of the room; this will result in a real investment in order to prevent unsanitary formations of mold also in view of the high levels of aqueous vapors created inside the bathroom itself.

HEATING SYSTEM

BATHROOM
Remodeling with an Architect

The heating system of our bathroom is a fundamental aspect capable of strongly affecting our living comfort. In the event that we are faced with a malfunctioning system or are simply looking for a better heating system, the possible solutions may be different. Tubular radiators, (also called towel warmers), could represent a space-saving alternative able to allow us to heat the environment as well as our bathroom towels - also saving on energy consumption. These wall-mounted radiators are generally composed of tubular bars available in different materials and sizes, moreover, according to our needs it is also possible to choose towel warmers that can be connected to plumbing, electrical or mixed systems. Alternatively, where the bathroom is part of a complete renovation project of your home, the installation of underfloor heating could represent a further possibility that can provide hygiene, temperature and, of course, living comfort benefits.

WATERPROOFING

The floors and walls of the bathroom are definitely put to the test by potential water infiltration. Therefore, correct waterproofing of the walls and wall coverings could prevent us from later (expensive) repairs, perhaps due to water infiltration in the underlying part of the shower or tub.

The advice is to waterproof not only the sanitary ware but also the walls and wall coverings, for example through the use of waterproofing sheaths and resins.

COMPLIANCE WITH CURRENT REGULATIONS

A correctly carried out bathroom renovation must certainly take into account the regulations in force in the construction field. Generally, most of the bathroom renovations do not require particular authorizations except, for example, the one that concerns interventions on the walls and / or related planimetric changes of the house. In both cases, these operations must comply with the types of regulations in force.

BATHROOM RENOVATION COST

It is undeniable this is a very important factor, in fact your budget will affect your restructuring, so before you start, do your calculations.

THE REAL PROBLEMS YOU WILL FACE IN BATHROOM RENOVATION

*A*ll the articles you will read always tell you the usual things: what are the trendy tiles, whether it is better to choose between free-standing or suspended sanitary ware, how beautiful the floor-level shower is, how a whirlpool bath gives an extra touch of luxury to your bathroom ... some (rare) articles in *which hypothetical examples are invented from scratch with equally hypothetical solutions ... Surely all very nice, but the reality is that you will not find any article that explains exactly the practical aspects of the design and construction of a bathroom. But these are the main aspects you should worry about right away when you decide to renovate your bathroom!*

The reasons why, before thinking about the tile, it is essential to think about facing all the practical aspects are simple:

If you don't want your new bathroom to turn into a lap pool, and you really want to get the most out of your bathroom remodel, the things you need to worry about are very different than the trendy tile and toilet. Especially if you don't want to risk doing damage (and when water is involved it's a very easy thing) that you will remember for life.

To carry out a bathroom renovation done in a workmanlike manner:

- Avoid doing work illegally
- The real problems you will face
- How the sanitary ware must be arranged and the minimum distances
- What are the finishes you can choose from?
- How much, at the end of the affair, it costs you to redo the bathroom

As you can see the most debated point in all the articles that talk about bathrooms, (finishes) I put in fourth place: only after solving the practical problems can you really take care of finishes. Also, because it is not uncommon for the interior layout you have chosen to affect the finishes (while the opposite is almost never the case).

START HERE: DO YOU KNOW WHAT IT REALLY MEANS TO RENOVATE A BATHROOM?

Most people believe that renovating the bathroom simply means changing the fixtures, perhaps moving them a bit because we are tired of how we have always seen them, and replacing the old tiles with more modern ones.

Do you also believe that this is the case? If your answer is yes, I'm sorry to give you the bad news: what we just talked about is barely a bathroom make-over. By "renovating" your bathroom in this way you will not solve any of the real problems that plague it.

TO UNDERSTAND THE REASON FOR THIS, YOU HAVE TO START FROM A QUESTION: WHY DID YOU DECIDE TO RENOVATE THE BATHROOM?

The answer is usually this: the bathroom is now so old that the tiles are all chipped and the joints are now black with mold, the toilet is encrusted and clogs up every time your child goes to the bathroom, there are so many in the tub layers of limestone that a stalagmite is forming, the mirror is losing pieces and every time you open the tap you risk being left with the tap in your hand...

These (and others) are the things that you can see and evaluate with the naked eye and that lead you to think that perhaps the bathroom is now old and needs to be redone. But think about it: if the finishes are obsolete, **won't everything underneath them and that you cannot see with the naked eye will be too?**

The essence of a bathroom is for the most part hidden: the essential part, the one that determines its functionality, you do not see because it is under the plaster or under the floor screed. But exactly as the tub becomes encrusted, so too do the pipes, the wells, the drains, wear out over time, and end up breaking and causing flooding (with the tenants on the floor below asking you for thousands in damages) and to force you to use cloths continuously if you do not want to go sailing in the bathroom.

So, replacing only the finishes will certainly make your bathroom beautiful but the continuous problems due to the advanced age of its structural components will remain unaffected. It would be like putting the body of a brand-new Ferrari on the mechanics (chassis, engine, gearbox, etc.) of a 1967 utility car. A disastrous result!

To answer the question, I posed to you earlier: renovating a bathroom means making a clean sweep of everything, including plants, screeds and plasters. Only in this way can you say that you have a new bathroom, made to perfection and that will not give you problems over time.

Now let's tackle the 5 points I listed above one by one.

DO NOT DO THE WORK ILLEGALLY!

Make sure you follow the rules in your region and find out if there are any tax breaks for bathroom renovations.

- THE REAL PROBLEMS YOU WILL HAVE TO FACE IN THE BATHROOM RENOVATION

The time has come to talk about the practical problems (or if you want to call them also technical) that will surely emerge during the works **but that you can very well foresee before they start!**

I want to reassure you: it is nothing dramatic and unsolvable, but if not taken into due consideration from the earliest stages it could give you unpleasant surprises (also and above all, economic).

PROBLEM 1: HOW MUCH SCREED DO YOU HAVE UNDER THE FLOOR?

*Y*ou've *probably walked into some recently remodeled bathroom inside a 30-40-year-old condominium. One thing you have surely noticed is that, somewhere, there is a step that divides the bathroom into two parts: one higher and one lower.*

This is by no means an aesthetic solution expressly desired by the client (although objectively almost always the effect is beautiful) but simply a solution adopted to solve a technical problem: the lack of sufficient space under the tiles to be able to pass the pipes of the installations.

Let's try to understand: all the sanitary fixtures in your bathroom are connected to both a water supply line (hot and cold) and a water drain to the sewer. This second line must converge towards what are commonly called drains: vertical ducts that convey all the waste water from the apartments of a condominium to the municipal sewer. Try to find it: probably in your bathroom, perhaps near the window, there is an enlargement of the wall, as if it were a column: that is not a supporting column but a conduit through which the pipe that collects all the drains of the apartments. Even your bathroom must necessarily convey all the waste water from the sink, bidet, toilet, shower / tub to that duct. And to do this, pipes are put under the floor.

The waste water discharge system works by gravity: that is, they go from top to bottom (unlike the water supply system which works by pressure). Therefore, to make sure that everything works correctly without the risk of it becoming clogged every day, the part of the plant responsible for disposal cannot be perfectly level but must have a minimum slope. Basically, the pipes you have under the floor cannot be perfectly horizontal but must be slightly inclined.

Furthermore, to ensure a better functionality of the whole system, the drains of the hygienic devices (with the exception of the toilet) are conveyed to a small circular drain which can be accessed in the event that some object accidentally ends up in the drain (how many rings have been saved from these wells!), or for any other type of obstruction / damage, simplifying and making all maintenance operations much cheaper. Starting from this well, a tube, which of course must always be sloping, is inserted into the drain column.

WHY IS THE TOILET NOT INSERTED INTO THIS WELL?

The pipe that comes out of the toilet has a larger diameter than the one that comes out of the other bathroom fixtures, I think it's easy to imagine why.

Therefore, it is not convenient to convey it to a well together with the other drains, but it is much more practical to introduce it directly into the drain.

 This whole set of systems consisting of pipes and a manhole is always positioned on the floor and, at its thickest point, usually reaches up to 15 centimeters. And here the problem arises: all buildings built up to no more than 20 years ago have always provided screeds with a thickness much less than 15 centimeters (in reality, even the new ones rarely reach these thicknesses). And the further back you go in time (so the older the building in which the bathroom is to be restored is) the more the thickness of the screeds decreases, to arrive at thicknesses equal to the minimum necessary to lay the floor (we are talking about only 3-4 cm). So, in these cases (and if your bathroom to be restored as it is probable is in a building with at least thirty years of life it is also your case) to be able to create a system that works well and that will not give you problems over time, you will almost certainly have to provide a step inside your bathroom.

The most common solution is to keep the part of the bathroom with the sink at the same height as the rest of the house, while the part with all the other sanitary fittings (toilet, shower / tub) is raised.

Of course, this does not have to happen always: a lot depends on when and how your property was built, but it is a probability that you must take into consideration.

In terms of costs, it does not very much, it is a few centimeters of light concrete, but it varies a lot in terms of aesthetics. And if I have to tell you all: dividing the bathroom into a low area and a high area often makes your bathroom much more beautiful. So, it is a technical necessity that translates into an aesthetic improvement.

PROBLEM 2. IS THE WALL THICK ENOUGH?

DOES THE TOILET YOU CURRENTLY HAVE IN THE BATHROOM HAVE THE DRAIN PAN POSITIONED AT THE TOP?

Or is it positioned in sight just behind the toilet? If the answer is yes, the wall on which it is fixed is probably not thick enough to allow the installation of a flush-mounted box.

In fact, among all the systems that are embedded in the walls that delimit the bathroom, the basin that contains the waste water is the element with the greatest thickness.

This basin is actually not very thick, usually around 10 centimeters (now even slightly less) but many years ago it was also used to build the walls of the bathroom with 8 cm thick bricks to which two layers of plaster were added to get to a thickness overall about 11 centimeters. You understand that in such a small thickness it is not possible to insert a concealed cistern if not risking that in the next room a lump will appear at the height of the toilet cistern!

So how to solve the problem of the unsightly visible cistern in this case? The solutions are there and they are various:

You could build a counterwall from the existing one made with thin boards 3 centimeters thick. You would then have a total thickness of 11 centimeters (in addition to the plaster), sufficient to place a built-in box

Create a light counterwall (gypsum) behind the only wc where all the tubes and the discharge cassette are. This way you avoid touching the back wall.

You could choose a toilet with an external box design. There are some very beautiful aesthetic solutions.

- THE CORRECT DISTRIBUTION OF SANITARY WARE IN THE BATHROOM

NOW COMES THE MOST INTERESTING PART: WHAT IS THE BEST ARRANGEMENT OF THE FIXTURES IN THE BATHROOM?

Of course, everyone will tell you: "it depends on the shape of your bathroom, every situation is different". This is not the case, in fact, if it is true that you have to adapt each solution to your specific case, there are small rules dictated by practice and common sense that I advise you to respect in order not to have bad results.

1. What do you need to see first when entering a bathroom?

When you enter a bathroom the first thing you see should NEVER be the toilet. It is true that we are talking about a bathroom but it must still be a decent and practical place: when you go to the bathroom you usually use the toilet, wash your hands and then go out. So, the closest thing to the door, or the first thing you see, should be the sink.

If you can't find any solution to put the sink near the door then try to put the bathtub or shower in it, which are often two beautiful objects to see. (Of course, if this is not possible, there is no law that forbids you to put the toilet in front of the door!)

2. *Where do you have to put the toilet?*

The ideal location is by the window. The reason I think you can figure it out for yourself: smells leave the room faster. Also, in this case it is not always possible, in any case try to put it as close as possible to the window. (In fact, it often happens that, for reasons of space, you are forced to put the shower or bathtub near the window. In this case, put the toilet next to the shower).

3. First the bidet or the toilet?

What I wrote in the previous paragraph should already give you an idea of what the ideal arrangement should be: first the bidet and immediately after the toilet.

Always remember one concept: try to put the thing that gives you the dirtiest feeling, the toilet, as far as possible from the entrance to the bathroom (of course I'm not telling you that your toilet is dirty!).

4. Where do I put the shower (or tub)?

There is no precise rule. The shower and the bathtub are one of the predominant elements in the bathroom (given the size) so there are two facts:

Wherever you put it, it's visible.

You never know where to put it (especially if the bathroom is not very big).

The best location would be in front of the bidet / toilet unit. However, this results in a considerable narrowing of the bathroom, which is often not desirable.

A second solution could be, in a narrow and long bathroom where all the fixtures are located along one wall, insert it between the sink (located near the bathroom entrance) and the bidet / toilet unit. In this solution you have to make sure that the space in front of the shower is large enough to pass through easily. We will explore the dimensions and distances in the next paragraph, but keep in mind that if you position the shower in this way, you need at least 60 centimeters to pass by easily. A third solution, which is the one that allows greater space optimization in many cases, is to insert the shower where you would never think: under the window. Even in this case is an optimal solution for narrow bathrooms and long, in fact unable to have a very large shower (as wide as the entire bathroom) and not from annoyance. The only precaution is to replace the window panes with frosted glass.

Two typical examples

Of course, there are many possible variables, and it all really depends on the shape and size of your bathroom, so an ad hoc solution must almost always be studied. But the small rules that I have listed above are valid in all cases and are perfectly suited to the two most common forms of bathrooms that can be found inside condominiums:

The narrow and long bathroom

The square bathroom

In reality, the first case (narrow and long bathroom) is clearly the most widespread form: almost all condominium apartments have a bathroom with these proportions since, being considered a service space, it is obtained by trying to waste as little space as possible in favor of the other main environments.

The ideal arrangement in the narrow and long bathroom.

If you need to renovate a bathroom of this type, the best solution is always to put all the sanitary ware on one wall. The best sequence is: sink, (bidet), toilet and shower / tub under the window.

THE IDEAL LAYOUT IN THE SQUARE BATHROOM

If, on the other hand, you have a square bathroom, the situation is a little different: of course, you cannot put all the sanitary ware on one wall but you will probably be forced to distribute them on two opposite walls.

Always remember, if possible, to put the bidet and toilet next to each other. If you don't have enough space, place the bidet and toilet opposite each other with the toilet next to the shower and the bidet next to the sink. These are of course all practical advice but remember that in any case it is the position of the entrance door and the drain that controls the arrangement of the sanitary ware: the closer to the drain the toilet is the less problems you will have.

5. The dimensions and the right distances of the sanitary ware

It is important that you know how much space you need around each piece of sanitary ware. For those who are not experts, it's easy to make mistakes by placing the sanitary ware too close to each other and thus making the bathroom difficult to use. These are simple ergonomic measures that will help you define the layout of your new bathroom in detail.

THE SINK

How big is a sink?

There are the standard sizes, i.e., those of the classic ceramic washbasin with the column underneath (about 60 centimeters wide by about 50 centimeters deep) and then there are the measures of what is now actually installed, i.e., designer sink tops, with the most disparate shapes and sizes.

If the bathroom you are renovating is the main one in your home, then the advice is to think of a sink surface about 90 centimeters wide and between 50 and 55 centimeters deep: it is certainly more comfortable.

As for the living space that must be on the sides, just think about how you use the sink: you put yourself in front of it.

Considering the standard sink, it is sufficient to leave 10 centimeters to the left and 10 centimeters to the right of the sink to allow optimal use. If, on the other hand, you want to opt for a more generously sized sink, you can easily ignore the space needed on the sides, indeed you could even lean it against a side wall without problems. Remember, however, if the sink is near the door, to check that it can open without bumping into it.

THE BIDET

The dimensions of almost all models of bidets and toilets are standard: 38 centimeters wide by 55 centimeters deep. From here it is a little different, unless you are looking for small bathroom fixtures for a very small bathroom.

For the space needed on the sides, even in this case, I invite you to think about how you use the bidet: you straddle it. So, when you think about how to put it in your bathroom you have to keep in mind that you need, on both sides, enough space to put your legs: 25 centimeters is more than enough space (unless you are 2 meters tall).

Keep in mind a detail that can help you save space:

- if the bidet is next to the sink and if the latter is the classic type (i.e., the one with the column below and not with a cabinet), the distance between the sink and the bidet it can be reduced to only 10 centimeters, because one leg will end up under the sink.

On the other hand, of course, you will need about 25 centimeters.

THE TOILET

We have already said about the dimensions when talking about the bidet, for the space instead the reasoning to be done is a little different.

The toilet can be used in two ways: if you are a man on some occasions, you put yourself in front of it (standing), in all other cases (men and women) you have to sit on it. Therefore, the strictly necessary space is that of the toilet itself. But for practicality it is always good to have at least 15 centimeters per side of free space. Clearly if on one side (as it is likely to be) there is the bidet, on that side you will have to have the 25 centimeters we were talking about above.

One thing you have to pay attention to is the space that must be in front of all these sanitary wares: the minimum space is about 60 centimeters.

Although this may seem small, keep in mind that these are objects that are located below your point of view, so you do not have the impression of being in a very narrow space as if you were in a corridor 60 centimeters wide. Having said that, the advice is to try to have at least 70-80 cm in front of these sanitary fixtures, to ensure greater comfort. If your bathroom is narrow, you can try to find a smaller model of toilet on the market: there are many and they are absolutely no more uncomfortable than the classic ones.

THE SHOWER (OR TUB)

In the case of a shower, you must always pay attention to a fundamental point: access to the shower must be free of any obstacles: I happened to find showers whose access was made practically impossible by the presence of a toilet right in front.

In this case you do not have space problems on the sides, indeed if you can lean it against two contiguous walls it is even better. The important thing is that there are at least 60 centimeters in front of the entrance door to the shower cubicle. Keep in mind that a standard shower is 80 × 80 centimeters in size, but it's easy to find smaller or rectangular ones. But always remember: a shower must never have any side smaller than 70 centimeters and in this case, it would be preferable that the second side is longer, to give more space inside.

For the bathtub, the matter is similar to the shower, although perhaps even simpler: make sure you have enough space to get in and that's it. Do you want to know the dimensions of a bathtub? I could answer you: any size you want. In fact, even the standard dimensions of a rectangular tub start from a tiny 120 × 70 cm to reach 200 × 90 cm. The most common in bathrooms in apartments is 180cm long x 70cm wide.

RENOVATION

If you decide to cover the floor and walls with tiles, remember that the tiles you will place on the ground must be non-slip and impact resistant. Wall tiles are usually of a softer clay that easily splinters (of course if something falls on them) and being often glazed when you bathe become slippery, risking a fall after a shower. Just ask the retailer to quickly resolve this possible problem.

If your bathroom is small, or it is narrow and long, I recommend that you put large tiles (60cm x 60cm) in order to give the impression that it is larger. Better if rectified, i.e., cut in such a way that they can be laid with an almost imperceptible gap between one tile and another. Clearly, the tiles with these characteristics cost significantly more than normal tiles, so don't expect to spend little and have high-quality materials. But keep in mind that the bathroom is usually small, so it is almost always a few hundred $ of extra material.

IS THERE ONLY CERAMIC FOR THE BATHROOM?

The answer, of course, is no: the idea that the bathroom floor and walls must necessarily be covered with ceramic tiles is wrong. It is true that mostly waterproof materials are needed (especially on the ground if you don't want to flood the downstairs tenant), but there are many other solutions.

I will mention only one that is currently having a good diffusion: resin, others we will see in other chapters. It is a material that is good in the bathroom as it is waterproof and therefore does not let water pass through the floor and protects the walls. It can also be obtained in an almost infinite quantity of finishes and being continuous, it manages to make your bathroom look much larger than it actually is.

HOW MUCH DOES IT COST TO RENOVATE THE BATHROOM?

Having made this necessary premise, let's understand what works (and costs) are necessary to renovate your bathroom:

Demolitions and disposal,

Masonry works,

Waterworks,

Electrical system,

Finishes and sanitary ware.

Let's see them one by one.

1. Demolition and disposal

Remember that here we are talking about refurbishing your bathroom, then:

- *remove all the fixtures and fittings,*
- *completely remove the tiles lining the walls,*
- *remove the plaster under the tiles,*
- *remove the floor tiles,*
- *remove the concrete screed that is between the tiles and the load-bearing floor slab,*
- *remove all the pipes of the systems that were inside the screed, as well as those that were in the walls.*

Of course, if you have to move walls you will need to add the demolitions of the existing walls.

In addition to being demolished, all this material will have to be transported to landfills and disposed of there.

So, in reality you will have to incur 3 costs:

Demolition

Transport

Disposal

Of course, the final cost of these operations depends on the amount of material and therefore on the size of your bathroom. I guess you don't want to start making complicated calculations to see how much each single phase of every single work you are going to demolish will cost you, so I give you some broad references to understand how much you will spend.

You only need two data: the floor area and the area of all the walls (to calculate it you just need to multiply the length of the wall by its height).

For all the demolition of plaster and tiles that you will do on the walls you will have to spend approximately $15 to $18 per square meter.

For all demolition of floors and screeds you will have to spend approximately $22 to $26 per square meter.

To remove and dispose of sanitary ware and related taps you will have to spend around $10 per piece.

If you have to change the shape and size of the bathroom to demolish entire walls you will have to spend between $20 and $22 per square meter.

DO YOU WANT TO KNOW A WAY TO SAVE SOMETHING?

If once you have removed the tiles from the walls, you see that the underlying plaster is in good condition, you can decide not to remove it but to do what is called "smoothing" to bring the walls back perfectly flat. In this way you save both the costs of demolition and disposal of the plaster and a large part of the costs of new plaster.

However, the best advice is always to redo all the plaster.

2. Water system

The water system must first be created, which consists of two parts: the water load (hot and cold) and the water discharge (that goes into the sewer). Let's consider a normal bathroom where there are:

A sink

A toilet

A shower / bath

The plumber will have to put a manifold in the bathroom: essentially inside a recessed box (usually hidden behind the door) he will bring the general hot and cold-water pipes and from here the pipes that go to each sanitary appliance will start. In addition to the work strictly necessary to create the system, you will also need to consider the necessary masonry works (creation of the niche and traces to pass the pipes to the wall). So, the costs you will incur will be:

Collector: from $200 to $300,

Loading and unloading lines for each appliance from $150 to $250 per appliance,

Masonry works: from $200 to $300,

On balance, a complete plumbing system for your bathroom will cost you from $1,000 up to $1,600

3. Electrical system

By completely redesigning the bathroom you will also be forced to redo the electrical system: in fact, the regulations currently in force are very different from the old ones. Fortunately, an electrical system for the bathroom consists of a few elements:

A ceiling light point,

A wall light point above the sink,

The switches to turn on the lights.

Some power sockets (usually no more than 2 or 3), one of which is of the Schuco type (commonly called "German") which must be positioned next to the sink. Being a small intervention, the total cost of an **electrical system for the bathroom hardly exceeds** $500, including the costs for creating the traces in the wall.

PS: Since the electrical system must be certified, check that the electrician who does it can issue the certification and above all that it complies with all the laws on the distances between electrical terminals (lights, sockets and switches) from the water supply points (taps).

4. Masonry works

After having made the systems, you need to move on to the construction work:

- *The screed in the floor including the creation of any steps,*
- *The plaster on the walls,*
- *Any masonry if you have moved any walls,*
- *Also in this case, as for demolitions, you will need the surface area of the floor and that of the walls.*
- *The average cost for a floor screed ranges from $20 to $30 per square meter.*
- *The average cost for plaster ranges from $18 to $25 per square meter.*
- *The average cost for brick walls ranges from $20 to $35 per square meter.*

5. Finishes and Sanitary Ware

Here you can give vent to your imagination: we have already said that the choice is infinite and you can find many articles that can give your ideas on this. Unfortunately, the prices of the finishes are also directly proportional to their quality. Let's see together what these finishes are:

Flooring,

Wall cladding,

Sanitary ware and taps,

Painting.

Here I will try to give you only broad reference average prices, but keep in mind, for example, that if you wanted to cover your bathroom with mosaic-like tiles you could end up, just for the supply, having to spend even over $100 per square meter. So, remaining with our feet on the ground, the items that make up the finishes are composed of two parts:

THE COST OF PURCHASING MATERIALS.

Floors and wall coverings: installation from $30 to $35 per square meter, supply of materials from $20 to $50 per square meter (medium / good quality materials).

Keep in mind that wall claddings almost never go up to the ceiling (unless you have special aesthetic needs) but often stop at the height of the door, that is 2.1m. The upper part will be painted.

HOW TO SAVE ON COATINGS.

A choice to save money is not to cover all the walls of the bathroom with tiles, but only those in direct contact with water (essentially those on which the sanitary fixtures are fixed). You can simply paint the others, making sure to use a suitable paint, possibly anti-mold. The same goes for the sanitary ware. In this case, the installation can be more expensive because it also includes the installation of the taps. So: *installation* from $80 to $120 *per piece, cost of bathroom fixtures* from $150 to $400 *per piece, taps from* $50 to $150 per piece. Finally, the painting: in fact, it will be essential to repaint the ceiling and the part of the wall not covered with tiles*. The cost here will not be high: between* $5 *per square meter and* $8 *per square meter (of course for standard finishes, if you are looking for special effects the cost goes up to over* $12 *per square meter).*

6. Various works

A small paragraph is missing: in fact, there are additional works that could give a final touch to your bathroom. One is certainly a false ceiling with the insertion of recessed spotlights. The cost in this case is between $30 and $40 per square meter, including spotlights.

CLEARING OUT THE BATHROOM

1) DISMANTLE THE OLD BATHROOM FIXTURES / FURNITURE AND CLEAR OUT THE BATHROOM

To be able to redo the bathroom it is necessary to disassemble everything, to disassemble the bathroom fixtures, just remove the screws that anchor them to the ground and tap them slowly until they detach from the ground. They are usually anchored to the ground by means of screws and white mastic, you have to be careful not to hit them too hard to avoid breaking them and also damaging the pipes.

2) REMOVAL OF TILES / FLOORS

If you are going to replace old siding and tiles with the help of a mallet and flat-tipped chisel, removing the tiles and siding is a pretty quick operation. With the mallet and the chisel just pry the tiles between the screed / wall and the edge of the tiles with small strokes. This is a tiring operation but with half a day a single person can easily dismantle the surface of a standard-sized bathroom.

3) REMOVAL OF THE OLD ADHESIVE

This operation is definitely the longest and most tiring, under the tiles you will find the old adhesive on top of the concrete screed, to do a good job you have to remove it all by uncovering the screed so that you can reposition the new tiles without raising the top. You have to very patiently hit the adhesive in various directions to remove it completely, it may take more than a full day for a large bathroom.

4) COLLECTION AND DISPOSAL OF WASTE

The waste produced by a renovation of the bathroom is bulky, it must be collected in special sacks for masons and disposed of at an authorized center, or free of charge at the ecological centre of your municipality.

IS IT NECESSARY TO REDO THE SCREED?

The lack of compactness and a flat and smooth appearance, the presence of visible or small and widespread cracks, and parts that detach from the substrate are the alarm bells that allow, even just looking, to understand that the screed has not been made completely correctly or as they say in construction, in a workmanlike manner.

nn.n1vn

Such "defects" in the screed must be eliminated and / or corrected. Continuing with the laying of the floor is a bold choice, especially if the floor will be glued, because all the problems previously detected in the support screed will affect the finish of the floor, with sometimes irreversible damage.

BUT HOW DO YOU KNOW IF A SCREED HAS BEEN MADE CORRECTLY?

Below is a brief description of the most common mistakes in making the screed.

SCREED WITH BLEEDING OR DUSTING

"Bleeding is a particular aspect of the segregation of concrete. It consists, in principle, in the rising to the surface of a part of the mixing water with the formation of a layer of water and cement on the surface of the conglomerate itself. The phenomenon may be the cause of an early degradation of the flooring."

If you try to scratch or engrave the screed with a steel nail, creating lines at a close distance between them, a solid and compact screed must not be able to be deeply engraved, it must not crumble as a result of the action of the nail and above all it must not show dusting. If, on the contrary, its 'dusts' or disintegrates or appears inconsistent and crumbly, we are dealing with a bleeding screed. It is important to know that a floor cannot be glued to this substrate, as the detachment of the flooring is very likely.

The bleeding layer must be removed, the surface must be cleaned and then a fixative primer must be applied to the inconsistent surface to regularize the screed.

SCREED WITH CRACKS

The surface is not uniform and smooth and has showy cracks, or many small but widespread cracks: we are in front of a screed with cracks. Cracks are caused by thermal and hygrometric shrinkage, due to incorrect quantities of water in the mixture, in excess or in defect. "The formation of cracks can also be attributed to high loads, to the deformation of the substrate or to the permanence of the screed in contact with the environment before laying the finishing layer or to inadequate curing".

In general, "a limited presence of cracks does not affect the quality of a screed, if these are of limited width", but if the cracks have a significant width or even if they are small, they are many and widespread, then it is necessary to intervene.

In the case of large and deep cracks, it is necessary to seal them with epoxy resins, while in the case of diffuse and superficial cracks, an anti-cracking desolidarizing layer could be applied.

SCREED WITH INCONSISTENT THICKNESS

If hitting the surface of the screed with a weight of about 1kg in different points you hear an "empty sound" then there will be problems of anchoring to the bottom. Also, in this case the problem is due to an incorrect mixture. If the inconsistency is limited to some portions, these can either be restored with the use of an additive to improve the mechanical and adhesion characteristics of cementitious mixtures, or consolidated with a consolidating primer. If, on the other hand, the inconsistency affects a large surface, then the screed must be demolished and rebuilt.

SCREED WITH CRACKS IN CORRESPONDENCE TO THE PIPES

This is the case in which the pipes of the systems emerge on the surface because they are not completely anchored to the bottom; The injuries are caused by the inadequate thickness of the screed above the pipes, ie when it is less than 3cm; or when, despite being aware of having reduced thicknesses, an electro-welded mesh is not positioned before casting. You can intervene by demolishing the screed on the sides of the lesion and resuming the casting, this time placing a metal mesh.

NON-PLANAR SCREED

If when placing a 250 cm straight edge on the screed, it is not perfectly planar to the support, the surface has both convex and concave irregularities. Non-flatness may be due to curing or incorrect installation. To restore the flatness, you can intervene with a primer and then with a level smoothing.

All the solutions seen so far to restore any damage to the screed can be adopted if the damage itself is not excessive, otherwise it will be necessary to seriously consider the possibility of demolishing and reconstructing the support screed correctly.

THE SCREED

The screed is the cementitious layer that is laid on the floor and is used to level the floors, bringing them to a desired height. The screed is also used to accommodate the pipes of the plumbing system, those of the heating (also with radiant panels) and electrical cables. Once the floors are covered, this layer will no longer be visible. It is important to do it well.

For the screed to be functional and made in a workmanlike manner, it must be flat and connect the rooms of a house in a coplanar way, allowing the doors to be opened. There must be no difference in height even when using different materials on the ground: between a tiled floor and one in parquet or marble there must be no difference. And again: it must not have slopes so as not to hinder the optimal support of the furnishings. Unfortunately, an error of a few millimeters in the execution of a screed is enough to be obliged to remedy it with additional interventions and costs. Risks include: doors that let in light from below or non-level cabinets that seem crooked compared to the surrounding walls. And these are just examples.

You need 4/6 centimeters for the screed: how to calculate it

The height of the screed varies according to the type of building and, in general, ranges from 4 cm to 6/8 cm. For higher thicknesses it is advisable to integrate with non-compressible lightening material (for example expanded clay) in order to avoid excessive weight, costs and drying times. To have a floor at the same height throughout the house, whatever coating you choose, you calibrate the thickness of the screed by referring to a height. Usually, you start from the entrance and mark a meter high on the wall calculated from the landing. This measurement is reported in all the rooms of the house using an infrared device and the blue "knock-trace" cables or a rubber tube that exploits the principle of communicating vessels.

SCREED LAID AD HOC

The screed must comply with the Uni En 13813 standard, which specifies the requirements for the materials of the screeds to be built for indoor flooring. In addition, a number of factors must be taken into account, in order for the execution to be perfect. We must not neglect the thickness of the materials to be installed, because they are different: resins and linoleum reach 5/7 mm in thickness, ceramics generally are around 1 cm, parquet has variable heights from 1 to 2 cm, while with stone it is easy to reach 2 cm or even 3 cm. The laying technique of the coatings (with glues, mortars or floating) and the degree of sensitivity to humidity that the chosen flooring can withstand also counts. Finally, in order for there to be no errors in laying the screed, the finish of the screed itself is important: after having compensated or created the appropriate slopes according to the needs, it must be smoothed to obtain a regular and defect-free surface.

TRADITIONAL PREPARATION

A traditional screed typically consists of three materials: cement, sand and water. The dosage of each of these varies according to the environment and the destination: whether it is indoor or outdoor, for civil or industrial purposes. Additives or other materials are then used, in addition to the typical ones, to increase the thermal, acoustic or resistance performance of the screed. For example: gravel or polystyrene to lighten; quartz to smooth the surface and make the screed more tenacious.

Those who have no experience in the construction sector might think that making a concrete screed is a prohibitive work and within the reach of professional operators only.

Making a floor of a few square meters, however, is a work within the reach of many, if you know the right precautions and do not lack patience or the desire.

All you need to have, to make a small concrete floor or concrete screed, are the main materials such as cement, sand, and gravel. The essential tools to use, on the other hand, are a concrete mixer (depending on the importance of the work to be carried out, even a small one could be fine) and the electro-welded mesh.

THE PROCEDURE FOR CREATING THE CONCRETE SCREED

If you do not know the proportions of the materials to be used in the space in which the concrete screed is to be cast, these proportions can be used to obtain a total volume of mix of approximately 66-67lt:

a 25kg bag of cement,

9lt water,

0-12 washed sand: about 85kg, corresponding to an apparent volume of about 52lt of wet sand,

11-22gravel: about 34kg, corresponding to an apparent volume of about 21lt.

It is always useful to have electro welded mesh sheets, which can be purchased from building materials dealers.

Once in possession of all the necessary materials, first of all, it is necessary to create a perimeter using wooden boards inside which the screed will be thrown. In this way, the concrete does not come out of the space in which it is intended to be poured. It is advisable to mark the boards in such a way that the level within which they can be filled with concrete is visible. After that, it is necessary to introduce the net so that each sheet overlaps with the neighboring ones for at least the length of a mesh, usually 20cm; in order to work effectively, the mesh should be placed at half the thickness of the casting and in any case, it must be raised from the bottom; for this reason, it is advisable to place it on pieces of gravel or on fragments of solid brick.

PREPARATION OF THE CEMENT

To prepare the concrete, it is advisable to load half of the mixing water into the rotating concrete mixer first, to which sand and cement are added in the proportions described above. Finally, the remaining water can be added to bring the mixture to the required workability. The indicated water dosage should be sufficient to obtain a fluid or super-fluid consistency.

A mixture with lower workability (plastic or semi-fluid) is difficult to lay and to compact effectively and will have voids and gravel nests while an excessive dosage of water will make the mixture not very durable or not very resistant.

Once the concrete has been mixed, before casting it inside the wooden planks structure, it is advisable to moisten the ground to prevent a substrate that is too dry from removing water from the still fresh mixture, thus favoring the formation of cracks. The concrete must be spread with the help of straight rails, rasps and rakes, making sure it is level.

For example, to calculate the screed for a 5 cm thick layer (50 mm) and an area of 40 m2. It is necessary to multiply these two indicators; get 2 cubic meters of the mixture; therefore, based on the 1:3 ratio, you need to know the required amount of cement and sand. In our case, we need 0.5 m3 of cement and 1.5 m3 of sand; to make it easier to calculate the amount of material, cubic meters must be converted to kilograms. The weight of one cubic meter of concrete is 1300 kg, which means that 0.5 must be multiplied by 1.3. You get 6.5, which is 650 kg.

This example clearly demonstrates how to calculate the quantity needed to purchase the materials needed to fill the floor. Be sure to consider the fact that in the process of preparation, the composition for pouring decreases in volume. This is the norm. It is better to buy a little more bag of cement, sand or other materials. To determine the amount of mixture per screen, we must remember that from 1 m3 of the mixture, 0.6 m3 of solution is obtained.

The ratio of all materials to water can be easily calculated using a special calculator. Furthermore, it is possible to calculate the required amount of self-leveling material to obtain a perfectly flat surface. Different mixtures for filling the floor are not cheap, so it is necessary to carry out all the calculations in advance, determine the exact number of consumables. It doesn't matter what you think about making a screed: from sandblasted concrete, DSP or sand. The correct calculation of the materials is a guarantee of a high quality and long-lasting surface.

Once you have decided on the type of screed, purchased all the necessary materials, you need to start preparing the floor surface. First of all, it is necessary to remove the old bond, if there is one. Then carefully clean the surface from dirt and dust. If desired, the cleaned floor can be primed, but this process is not necessary. The thickness of the screed is important both in the apartment and in a private house. The degree of thermal insulation depends on this indicator. The thickness may vary depending on the selected materials and the area of the room, but do not forget to take into account that the incorrectly selected screed may be of poor quality.

Before proceeding with the installation of the screed, it is necessary to install beacons around the perimeter. With their help, you can fill the floor as smoothly as possible. If additional support is required, do not use wooden blocks. Under the influence of moisture, they deform. When installing a semi-dry screed on the walls, the doors and the insulation material of the partitions are laid.

Then proceed to the preparation of the mixture. This process depends on the materials you will be using. The main thing - to keep the proportions.

Once the casting operations have been completed, it is necessary to wait for the concrete to start setting; with usual cements this occurs after about 1½-2 hours at a temperature of 20 °. Higher temperatures accelerate setting and hardening while lower temperatures slow down the reaction. Concrete should not be cast at temperatures below 5 ° C.

In the hours following the casting, the concrete begins to set and hardening begins. In the first few hours, while the concrete is setting, it is still possible to further reinforce the surface with an anhydrous cement armor that can be incorporated into the screed by troweling.

A too quick drying, especially in the summer season, can lead to the formation of unwanted cracks that appear a few hours after casting. Excessive ventilation or insulation can cause the mixing water to evaporate before it has been able to complete the hydration of the cement. It is therefore essential to keep the surface moist for the first few hours, for example by spraying water on the surface. Avoid direct water jet that would ruin the surface at the point of contact.

Hardening of the concrete is a long process; ideally you should wait a month or at least a week before carrying on work.

Drying times

To lay ceramic floors (including terracotta, stoneware, stone, marble and anything else that does not suffer from humidity), it is necessary to wait at least 10 days after making the screed.

For parquet, linoleum, resins and laminate, the surface is considered ready for laying the covering only when the humidity of the substrates has reached levels below 2% throughout the thickness.

New premixed products

Sometimes very specific to solve particular situations, almost all the products on the market today to make the screed are ready-to-use premixes, to which just add water is enough. The most marketed products are divided into two categories: rapid and semi- rapid. The performances are such as to allow the achievement of the complete curing of a 5 cm substrate in just 7 days for the rapid ones; in 20 days for semi-rapid ones.

BATHROOM FINISHES

Furnishing the bathroom does not only mean choosing tiles and bathroom fixtures. For an optimal result, particular attention must also be paid to the combinations of materials and colors, finishes and coatings.

We don't just think about the walls and floors: in a bathroom design project we can also decide the finishes of the furnishings by choosing from many combinations to create a unique effect.

The options proposed are many and it can become complicated to disentangle among many materials, colors and styles. So here is a brief guide to orient yourself in the choice of bathroom finishes.

5 TIPS FOR CHOOSING BATHROOM FINISHES

Minimal, elegant or modern: whatever style you want to characterize your bathroom with, here are 5 tips that are always valid for choosing the finishes of the furnishings:

- Carefully consider the space available;
- Decide on the arrangement of the furniture and bathroom fixtures;
- Choose the style of the bathroom;
- Focus attention on the final result;
- Don't forget the lighting.

1. CAREFULLY CONSIDER THE SPACE AVAILABLE

When approaching a furnishing project, it often happens to underestimate the size of the bathroom. Instead, it is precisely from here that the reflection for the choice of the right materials and the most suitable colors must start.

In the case of a small bathroom, for example, we can opt for light colors that make the room airier. If, on the other hand, we have a larger space, we can venture with darker tones and more accentuated color combinations.

2. DECIDE ON THE ARRANGEMENT OF THE FURNITURE AND BATHROOM FIXTURES

Depending on how we decide to arrange the bathroom fixtures, the shower tray and the furniture, we will obtain different effects that we could complete with the right finishes.

For example, we could play with colors, combining contrasting tones to highlight the furniture on the walls. Or match the color of the top with that of the floor to create harmony in the room.

3. CHOOSE THE STYLE OF THE BATHROOM

After considering the available space and the placement of the furniture, we move on to the choice of furniture and finishes. The chosen style and the desired result play a fundamental role in this step. If we want to achieve a minimal and modern effect, we prefer neutral colors. We paint the walls white or beige and give continuity to the furniture finishes. The evaluation of the finishes, therefore, cannot ignore the choice of style.

4. FOCUS ATTENTION ON THE FINAL RESULT

Whether you are renovating an existing bathroom or furnishing that of your new home, it is very important to focus attention on the aesthetic and functional result you want to achieve. For example, the bathroom must also be furnished according to the use that will be made of it; both the arrangement of the furniture and the more or less delicate materials must be chosen according to the composition of the family unit.

5. DON'T FORGET THE LIGHTING

Fundamental in the choice of materials and colors of the finishes is also to consider the type of lighting we have.

Does the bathroom have a window or other sources of natural light? Do we have many light points or a single light point? Depending on the answers, you can opt for more delicate finishes or bold colors and materials such as marble or dark wood.

Mirrors play a very important role in lighting, both for the refraction of light and for the possibility of choosing backlit mirrors. There are many options to choose from, depending on whether we want to make the room extremely bright or create plays of light.

Bathroom finishes: we combine elegance, modernity and functionality

Thanks to these tips you can choose the finishes of your bathroom with more awareness. Thanks to the many solutions and the almost infinite possibility, it will be so easy to combine elegance, modernity and functionality in your bathroom.

COSTS AND TIMING

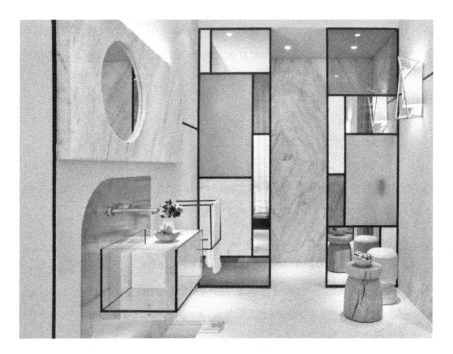

Housework always involves a certain amount of stress, and problems arise especially if it is the first experience with the renovation. For this reason, if you are struggling with the renovation of the bathroom, here are the times to keep in mind for this type of intervention.

Before dwelling on the time needed to renovate a bathroom, it is necessary to be aware of the different phases that make up the bathroom renovation: do you already know what you are going to face when starting the work on your bathroom?

BATHROOM RENOVATION: TIMING

There is no standard time frame for the renovation of a bathroom, each intervention will require more or less time depending on the work that the bathroom needs.

However, we can hypothesize some cases ...

In the restyling of a bathroom that is not too dated, the workers can take from 2 to 5 days, while if your bathroom has leaks or it is essential to replace important components such as the plumbing, then the work can last even 6 or 7 days. On average, bathroom renovations almost never exceed 7 days.

Among the different types of work in the house, the renovation of the bathroom is the one that certainly causes the most inconvenience to those who live there, passing through some delicate phases that prevent its use.

Not being able to use the bathroom is a problem, and it is precisely for this reason that the different phases of intervention must be organized, trying to minimize the impact this can have on the people living in the house.

Let's start from the basics: there are different degrees of intervention to which a bathroom can be subjected when we talk about renovations. Let's see the main ones, trying to understand their characteristics also in terms of expenditure.

Moving or creating from scratch - We are faced with the most complex and expensive case, that is to create a bathroom from scratch or move the previous one to a different location in the home. To obtain the desired result, you must necessarily touch other areas of the house, increasing costs.

Total renovation - In other words, when the renovation involves: demolition of portions of masonry, laying of tiles, moving of plumbing and electrical systems, replacement of sanitary ware. Put simply, completely redo an existing bathroom.

Partial renovation - A minor intervention, without masonry work, which involves only coatings, sanitary ware and related systems. We are faced with the recurring type of work of those who want to redo a bathroom and expect not to spend an excessive amount, relying on false beliefs such as: "It's just a sink and a shower" and "a friend of mine did it with a few $"; better to do the math well, because the factors that can drive up prices, as we will see, are many.

Renovation and relook – A less invasive intervention that should make you spend less working only on painting, choice of furnishings, replacement of sanitary ware without plumbing and lighting improvements.

In fact, the tiling remains, which would make the intervention fall into the previous category; in place of the tiler's job, however, it is possible to include in the relook of a bathroom the laying of low-thickness ceramics and vinyl materials that can be applied directly on existing tiles and floors.

This clear division is useful to have a yardstick when you go to talk to a professional, but we will never find these terms in an official proposal because the total cost of renovating a bathroom depends on too many factors to be simplified in this way.

WHAT AFFECTS THE BATHROOM RENOVATION COST?

Square footage

It might seem strange and not very logical, but the difference in square meters does not affect the cost to be considered to redo a bathroom. Of course, we will need more tiles and more paint for the walls when dealing with larger rooms, but the bulk of the shopping will come from other elements such as systems or furnishings, as we will see in the next points.

Installations

The bulk of the expense in the renovation of the bathroom is decided by the renovation works. In fact, working on pipes and manifolds means going to work on floors and walls, in case of problems with the general plumbing of the apartment, even outside the bathroom.

The technical characteristics of the system - with single or double pipes, in PVC or steel, with one or more manifolds - do not count for much in terms of expenditure, the problem is how much of the entire network of pipes and connections will have to be redone.

Let's take for example a new apartment with manifolds, pipes, distribution columns and drainage wells in the right position: in this case the intervention will only concern the connection of the sanitary ware and the testing. Different case: that of an old independent house where it was decided to move the bathroom;

here the whole system will have to be put back into operation by working on walls, floors and, in the worst case, also on the main pipes that carry water from the building's water network.

It goes without saying how much the presence or absence of masonry work affects the cost of a plumbing system which, as we have seen, can transform a simple partial refurbishment into a real construction site, consequently increasing costs.

Materials

The objects that you can install in a bathroom are more or less always the same: sink, cabinet, tub / shower, bathroom fixtures, lights, tiles, accessories and little else. Yet, for each one, the cost can drastically change even just for the material used, economic or valuable:

- chipboard / solid wood
- laminate / stone
- industrial terracotta / porcelain
- plastic / crystal

You pay for quality, and this applies to the choice of materials as well as to those who make the supplies, as we will see in the following point.

FURNISHINGS

We talked about redoing a large or small bathroom, completely or partially, with materials of different qualities; now all that remains is to face an expense item that can greatly increase costs: the choice of the manufacturer of accessories, bathroom fixtures and furnishings.

On the one hand, we can choose the quality, design and reliability of internationally known manufacturers, brands whose models appear in print and online magazines as examples of the best bathroom furniture. On the other hand, we have the same types of furnishings and accessories, only in the large DIY store version.

The economic difference between the two alternatives can vary a lot, and not only for the quality of the materials, which we have already talked about, but also for the accuracy in the construction and the research of the design.

Regardless of the quality, the function of furnishings and accessories remains unchanged - you can brush your teeth, take a shower and everything else - but the performance and personal appeal change over time.

A good product will tend to remain in good condition over the years and will be a pleasure to see every day, perfectly integrated into the overall look of your bathroom. You will then have a wide variety of choice between the different manufacturers, something that is lacking with mass production, which tends to standardize variants, models and sizes to reduce costs.

IS IT POSSIBLE TO RENOVATE A BATHROOM YOURSELF WITHOUT RESORTING TO PROFESSIONALS?

W*ould you like to restore your old bathroom yourself? Let's see if it is possible and how much it costs.*

Restoring the bathroom, useful tips

Redoing the bathroom is an expensive job and if entrusted to specialists, on average, it costs around 5 thousand $ for a standard bathroom without too many fine finishes such as whirlpool tubs or particularly well-finished shower cabins.

Removing old coatings, tiles, bathroom fixtures, fixing the water and electricity systems is certainly not a job that can be done in a day.

Is it possible to renovate the bathroom by yourself?

Theoretically it is possible since replacing the tiles and sanitary ware is part of ordinary maintenance, so it is not necessary to have special permits, in any case it is better to inquire in order to avoid having problems with neighbors especially due to the noises during the removal of the tiles. It must be calculated that doing a DIY bathroom is a very long operation compared to what professionals would do, you need to learn several things and have time to solve unexpected events.

Costs for cladding and flooring

They can be very varied, starting from 5 $ per square meter up to and even over 30 $, depending on your tastes. On average the tiles have little impact on the final cost since the bathrooms are small rooms compared to the rest of the house.

Costs for health care

Here too there are many choices that can cost from 30/40 $ for the made in China models up to and over 500 $ for the fine models, according to your tastes, you will choose the design that suits you best.

Washbasin and furniture

They can cost over 1000 $, but there is something for all budgets starting from about 200 $ for the simpler models even less, this also depends a lot on your preferences, a tour in all the do-it-yourself centers will certainly be able to clarify your ideas.

Disposal of waste

To dispose of the old tiles / sanitary ware you need to find an authorized center. This service is generally free, provided by every collection center in every municipality, and there are always those who need rubble to build if you notice a construction site in your vicinity you can try to find out if they need material to fill.

Redoing a do-it-yourself bathroom costs little, if you choose an economic solution, even less than 1000 $ could be enough, however the help of a plumber is usually recommended at least for the professional assembly of sanitary ware, taps, drains and any changes to the water system, a professional could put it all up in less than a day once everything else was prepared.

WE LIST THE MAIN OPERATIONS TO BE CARRIED OUT.

1) **Dismantle the old bathroom fixtures / furniture and clear out the bathroom**

To be able to redo the bathroom it is necessary to disassemble everything, to disassemble the bathroom fixtures just remove the screws that anchor them to the ground and tap them slowly until they detach them from the ground, you have to be careful not to hit them too hard to avoid breaking them and also damaging the pipes.

2) **Removal of tiles / floors**

Remodeling with an Architect

If you are going to replace old siding and tiles with the help of a mallet and flat-tipped chisel removing the tiles and siding is a pretty quick operation. With the mallet and the chisel just pry the tiles between the screed / wall and the edge of the tiles with small strokes. This operation must be done in the floor after having destroyed one.

3) Removal of the old adhesive

This operation is definitely the longest and most tiring, under the tiles you will find the old adhesive on top of the concrete screed. To do a good job you have to remove it all by uncovering the screed so that you can reposition the new tiles without raising the top. You have to very patiently hit the adhesive in various directions to remove it completely, it may take more than a full day for a large bathroom.

4) Collection and disposal of waste

The waste produced by a renovation of the bathroom is bulky, it must be collected in special sacks for masons and disposed of at an authorized center.

5) Laying the tiles

Making a floor is a simple operation but if you have no experience you have to pay close attention, you have to lay the tiles in an order established according to your aesthetic preferences, using adhesive and cutting the tiles with precision.

6) Assembly of the new sanitary ware

At this point it is necessary to do the opposite to disassembly, that is to reposition them in their established places, taking care to properly mount the gaskets, make the holes to anchor the sanitary fixtures to the ground, screw them in.

In conclusion: The bathroom is not exactly a job suitable for DIY unless you have a second bathroom available, a lot of patience and the desire to learn. To make a DIY bathroom it could take us even more than a week and often for those who do not have all this time it is better to resort to professionals or at least to help for the most delicate parts.

EXAMPLE OF A DIY BATHROOM MAKEOVER EXPENSE:

- Bathroom upholstery: 200 $
- New sanitary ware: 300 $
- Shower plate and shower cabin: 250 $
- New taps: 300 $
- Washbasin with cabinet: 200 $
- Pieces of pipe, fittings, gaskets: 50 $
- 80 l water heater: 90 $
- Help of a Plumber: 200 $

HOW TO RENOVATE THE BATHROOM WITHOUT REMOVING THE TILES

The bathroom is one of the most used rooms in the house, as it is used regularly several times a day. For this reason, in addition to ordinary maintenance, deeper restructuring interventions may be necessary.

Among the most frequently used solutions is the replacement of tiles - which in the bathroom, unlike any other domestic environment, cover a large part of the walls and therefore strongly characterize the aesthetics of the environment - for the installation of a new coating.

However, there are several alternatives to renovate the bathroom without removing the tiles or demolishing the flooring, let's see how.

COVER THE TILES: RESIN OR CONCRETE

There are two different approaches to cover the bathroom without removing the tiles; the first consists of covering the pre-existing coating with an elastic covering (resin or cement) while the second involves applying a second layer of thinner (and therefore lighter) tiles on the tiles already fixed to the masonry in order to create a new coating ceramic applied to the existing one.

If you decide to cover the old coating with a new resin or cement coating, it is necessary to carry out a series of preparatory interventions in order to ensure that the resin or cement adheres perfectly to the surface.

The first thing to do is to clean the joints, removing the residues of dirt that tend to accumulate in the spaces between the individual tiles; for this purpose, you can use a scraper or a sheet of sandpaper (passing it in profile) and a suitable detergent.

It is then necessary to clean the tiles with a specific product to eliminate the grease residues that could create adhesion problems. Once this is done, to even out the surface, it is possible to fill the joints with a primer.

Once these preparatory activities have been completed, a primer is applied, usually an epoxy resin; after the first coat of resin, before it dries, you need to spread a plastic mesh and fix it by spreading a second (thinner) layer of resin with a roller, making sure there are no irregularities.

To finish the job, two more steps are needed: the first involves the application of a layer of cement resin that makes the surface smooth and homogeneous and gives the color and material effect; the second consists of the surface finish which, in addition to protecting the underlying layer, also serves to give the desired more or less glossy aesthetic effect.

Resins can be used, as well as cement, to cover not only wall coverings but also bathroom floors; on the market there are self-leveling liquid resins and cementitious resins that can be smoothed or spatulated after application.

For those who do not want to give up a ceramic tile covering, there is an alternative solution, namely the installation of other tiles on top of those already present. In this case, it is good to opt for thin tiles, so as to minimize the particularly unsightly additional thickness near the door but also on the walls.

Thin porcelain stoneware tiles have a very reduced thickness - from 3 to 6mm - and are sometimes reinforced by a glass fiber mesh applied on the back. These thin tiles are available in many different formats and with decorative effects of all kinds: from stone, to wood, to colored and decorated surfaces: they are therefore perfect for combining aesthetics and the characteristics of resistance and cleanability typical of stoneware.

To lay this type of product, it is necessary to check that the old coating is solid and has been previously cleaned and degreased; the new tiles must then be applied with a suitable adhesive, making sure that the adhesive adheres well to the entire rear surface of the tile so as not to leave gaps underneath.

Alternatively, it is possible to renew the bathroom coverings using double-fired tiles, a different but equally versatile and practical material.

As for the laying of a new floor directly on top of the old one, the precautions are similar; the tiles cannot be too thin - as they are subjected to greater mechanical stress - nor too thick, otherwise the surface would be too high and this could cause practical problems.

But how to choose the most suitable material? For bathrooms, porcelain stoneware floors are generally preferred which, in addition to being able to almost completely resist water absorption (an essential factor in the bathroom), offers a wide range of solutions, both suitable from the point of view technical - high resistance and robustness - both on the aesthetic front.

The surface of the stoneware tiles, in fact, have various decorations that imitate the texture of the staves of wooden floors or the appearance of stone tiles: for this reason, they lend themselves to a wide range of applications and can be used for the realization of bathrooms in very different styles.

Redoing the bathroom without removing the tiles does not necessarily imply the remaking of the coverings or flooring (unless it is essential). In many cases, in fact, it is possible to obtain a good result by intervening in a less radical way. One of the solutions, in this sense, is represented by the renewal of the bathroom furnishings, the elements that more than others tend to deteriorate due to constant use.

Changing the furniture is a good option even if the wall tiles and flooring are recent and in good condition and, more importantly, they form a good 'neutral' basis for installing new furniture. The rules to follow for an optimal choice are the same ones to follow for any renovation or for the construction of a new bathroom: first of all, the stylistic coherence between the various components that will be installed in the environment must be respected; which is why each element must have an identity compatible with that of the other furnishing objects to which it will be combined.

Secondly, it is necessary to keep in mind what are the colors and shades of the floor and the tiles on the walls (whether they are the 'original' ones, or whether it is the resin or concrete coating applied on top: the combinations must not be neither too uniform (color on color) nor too strident (strong chromatic contrast) because the final result would be anonymous or disharmonious. The best solution is the compromise, that is a harmonious and balanced contrast between different colors able, at the same time, to enhance the individual pieces of furniture and the overall set-up.

Another aspect to take into consideration, beyond the aesthetic one, is the purely functional one: the furniture must not be large or bulky (because that would be impractical) but should be proportionate to the space available and to the overall dimensions of the bathroom, optimizing its functionality.

Choosing, for example, suspended furniture and sanitary ware facilitates cleaning operations while a heated towel rail allows, at the same time, to have a heating device and an additional support for towels.

These assessments are of particular importance because a renovation of the bathroom that does not involve interventions on the masonry structures - and consequently the possibility of remodeling the systems - does not allow to move the bathroom fixtures and furniture; therefore, having to keep the same distribution of the furniture, the latter must be able to improve the practicality and functionality of the whole environment, making the most of the available spaces.

STUDYING NEW LIGHTING

The final touch to renovating your bathroom without removing the tiles and floors is the lighting. Without masonry interventions it is not possible to expand the sources of natural light (if present) or to obtain new ones, so as to improve the daytime exposure of the whole environment. On the other hand, the installation of new lighting devices can significantly improve the overall effect of the renovated furnishings and, at the same time, make the bathroom airier and more functional.

In the bathroom, there are at least two points of light: one on the mirror that surmounts the sink unit and one in the center of the ceiling that illuminates the whole room; in both cases, the projection of the light beam must be implemented by means of bathroom lamps or spotlights capable of adequately illuminating the entire environment, especially if it has no windows, and to enhance the characteristics of the new coatings and furnishings. There are also mirrors equipped with integrated lighting elements, which help to improve the level of lighting in the bathroom, also creating a pleasant aesthetic effect.

HOW TO FURNISH A SMALL BATHROOM WITH 10 TRICKS

Y ou don't necessarily need large square footage to design an attractive and impactful bathroom.

With these simple tricks to furnish a very small bathroom, you will add sophistication and style to even the smallest of sizes. And remember that a small bathroom is much more practical for everyday life - it's easier to clean and heats up faster than large rooms.

BATHROOM
Remodeling with an Architect

1. Extra-small washbasin

2. Suspended sink

3. Large mirror

4. Stratified lighting

5. Light colored tiles

6. Optimized vertical space

7. Mix of textures

8. Glass shower doors

9. Wicker container baskets

10. Quirky wallpaper

Tricks for decorating a very small bathroom:

1. Extra-small washbasin

Opt for a small cabinet that develops in height. Create visual continuity with a mirror of the same geometric shape.

To optimize the use of available space, we recommend that you choose an element with several integrated storage solutions. This will make it easier for you to sort and organize cosmetics and toiletries.

2. Suspended sink

A suspended washbasin cabinet is the most suitable solution in very small bathrooms because in confined spaces the golden rule is to respect the proportions to the millimeter and leave as much space as possible without clutter.

Opt for a suspended wall sink - it frees up floor space and gives the room a more open look. To store bathroom accessories and products, you can also install a shelf between the sink and the mirror.

3. Large mirror

Mirrors are a functional element in the bathrooms of our homes and their use is one of the most popular tricks when it comes to visually enlarging very small rooms.

Mirrors, due to their reflective nature, add depth and create the optical illusion of greater amplitude. Choose a large one to place over the sink so that it covers a good part of the wall.

4. Stratified lighting

When choosing the lighting system for your very small bathroom, make sure that the room is illuminated evenly. Therefore, opt for a layered lighting scheme by playing with elements at different heights.

Uses a mix of shades of light, from the warmest of the wall sconces to the colder one of the ceiling lights.

5. Light colored tiles

Light colors have the power to visually enlarge tiny spaces. Use preferably white tiles and integrate a row of decorative additional tiles in the middle of the wall.

Doing so will bring visual interest to the overall look. On the contrary, the bathroom would be too bare without them.

For an even more distinctive effect, consider using clear three-dimensional shaped tiles that add a designer touch and an interesting dimension to your bathroom.

6. Optimized vertical space

When furnishing a small bathroom, try to maximize the vertical space. You can take advantage of suspended shelves, and wall cubes.

Alternatively, you can opt for creative solutions such as vertical elements in the shape of stairs leaning against the wall, with various shelves to be decorated with bath linen, prints and various objects.

7. Mix of textures

Don't be afraid to be daring in your small bathroom: gloss tiles on the wall that contains the bathtub, tiles with a matte finish on the floor and a whimsical shower curtain.

Stick to one or two reference colors when mixing different textures.

8. Glass shower doors

A good rule of thumb when furnishing very small bathrooms is to leave the space as visually open as possible. In these cases, transparent glass shower doors come in handy that do not block the light, allow the eye to look at the entire room without visual interruption and to perceive it as larger, airy and brighter.

9. Wicker container baskets

Wicker storage baskets are a trendy but above all functional piece of furniture when it comes to furnishing small spaces because they help keep order without cluttering too much.

They are elegant and versatile, adapting to bathrooms of any type and style. You can buy them in different shapes and sizes, alone or in sets. On the market they are coordinated for every budget.

10. Quirky wallpaper

A very small bathroom is the perfect place in the house where you can give free rein to your creative soul. Experiment with unexpected color or quirky wallpaper.

In this way you will not only give character to the environment but also distract attention from the small size of the space because the wall becomes the real protagonist.

Be sure to offset these colorways and textures with bright accents and a predominantly white decor scheme.

SHOWER OR TUB?

S hower or bath? This seems to be the question of the century, an eternal challenge between relaxation and practicality.

Every time a total renovation of the bathroom is carried out, this is the Hamletic doubt that grips anyone, as the choice will inevitably affect the organization and furnishing of the entire environment. Of course, the best choice would be to not give up either of the two alternatives, but this is not always possible. Small spaces, small and narrow rooms, only one bathroom available: what to choose in these cases? Shower or bath? Choose consciously.

BATHROOM
Remodeling with an Architect

Everything related to domestic environments, beyond aesthetics and personal taste, should be influenced by a single and very important factor: that is, one's own needs and requirements. Before proceeding with this important choice then ask yourself a series of questions:

- ❖ How many times a day do I dedicate myself to my personal hygiene by washing?
- ❖ How much time do I have daily to devote myself to my personal hygiene?
- ❖ Are there elderly people or people with mobility impairments at home?
- ❖ Are there any children in the house or am I going to have them?
- ❖ How much space is available?

These are just one example of ritual questions that should be considered before changing and renovating a bathroom. But not only: these questions can and must be asked every time you decide to change any other home environment, as these simple issues, if underestimated or not taken into consideration, can have important and unpleasant negative feedbacks that will lead you to feel unhappy in your own home. Is it worth feeling strangers or unsuitable in your own home so as not to give up an aesthetic factor or real estate embellishment? Remember that your needs and requirements must always be put first!

BATHS: THE PROS AND CONS OF CHOOSING

Return home after a stressful day at work and let yourself be pampered and indulge in relaxation with a nice hot bath, scented candles, background music and why not? also a nice glass of red wine. Here this is definitely the first image that appears in anyone's mind as soon as the word bathtub is mentioned. But if the idea of relaxation and comfort that only a hot bath can give makes your eyes shine and warms your heart, it is good to take into consideration even the most uncomfortable features before embarking on a hasty choice that will make you dissatisfied over time.

A bathtub is absolutely not recommended in an environment that is too small and narrow: always remember that you must be able to move easily and freely in your bathroom! Tubs take up a large volume of space, unlike the showers as we will see below, and therefore can significantly reduce the habitability and livability of your room.

In addition, bathtubs are not recommended for those who are always in a hurry and need to get "a wash on the fly": do you have any idea how long it takes a bathtub to fill? And are you really sure that once you are fully immersed in wellness you will have the strength and the courage to stay there for no more than two minutes? Another sore point is given by the consistent consumption of water that is used to fill a tub and therefore to wash, a consumption four times higher than that of a shower. If on the one hand, therefore, the bathtub will help you to give yourself pleasant moments of relaxation for the body and mind, on the other hand it could create stressful situations in your wallet for really high bills.

The practicality discourse deserves a separate note. While the bathtub is the ideal solution if you have children, as it allows you to wash the little ones in a quick and fun way, especially for them, using specific products for the care of infants. On the contrary, if there are elderly people or people with mobility difficulties in the house, a standard bathtub is not at all a solution to be taken into consideration. In fact, for this category of person, climbing over the edge of the pool to immerse themselves or even to get out of it, as well as being really difficult, could represent a real risk of falls that can result in unpleasant situations. To overcome this problem, nowadays you can enjoy the bathtubs equipped with a side or front door and seat that also allows the elderly to enter and exit the bathtub without any difficulty. If one of your concerns is the loss of water that could occur, rest assured: these tanks equipped with a door have been built and designed for this purpose, so you will not have any unpleasant water loss if you are careful with small precautions on entering before filling the tub and if you exit when it is completely emptied, as well as guaranteeing a good and careful maintenance of the gasket edges that make the bathroom structure waterproof.

One of the most beautiful features of the bathtub is that it is not only linked to the bathroom, but can really be used as a means of furniture in other rooms of your home, such as the living room or bedroom. Have you ever seen the movie Scarface? A bathtub, perhaps complete with a whirlpool, placed in the living room of your home could really be a pleasant surprise for your guests. So, you can transform your stay into a relaxation area / fun area with the inclusion of a mini swimming pool with hydromassage. Maybe the idea might be a little expensive, but you want the beauty of enjoying a nice bath while watching your favorite movie or your beloved TV series on a big screen? Or a bathtub, perhaps in a jacuzzi style, can be placed in the bedroom and could be ideal for enacting erotic hot fantasies with your partners. Or it could even be a real relaxation solution before letting yourself go into a deep night's sleep. Hot baths are known to help you relax and sleep better. If you have insomnia problems why not try it?

The market today allows you to choose from many types of bathtubs that differ in models and materials used for their construction. In fact, you can opt for rectangular, round, oval or quadrangular bathtubs, built-in or free standing, in ceramic, resistant plastic or various metals that adapt perfectly to your tastes and to the structure and furnishings of the premises. For example, for furnishings in Victorian style, art deco or early twentieth century, the bathtub becomes an indispensable must have, especially the free ones that rest on well-worked feet that recall the basics of the furnishing style.

SHOWERS: THE PROS AND CONS OF CHOOSING

When you think of the shower, the first adjectives that come to mind are: practicality, speed and space-saving. In fact, showers, unlike bathtubs, can take up very little space and therefore are really the ideal solution for those who have an environment that is small or narrow. In addition, there are corner showers that are positioned at an angle at the level of the bathroom walls in order to save you even more in terms of space.

But if with the shower you save in terms of space, this saving is made even stronger by a substantial saving in the bill: usually a shower lasts about 5 minutes, this will allow you to consume a much smaller amount of water compared to the consumption that requires a bathtub to be totally filled.

A shower is the best solution for those who often have little time, a hasty life or want to wash quickly, without giving up good personal hygiene.

Furthermore, showers are really the best solution for elderly people or people with mobility problems, as they can be equipped with appropriate seats, maintenance handles and anti-slip strips, thus becoming a practical means to ensure the cleanliness of all family members.

Very often when we talk about showers and bathtubs in comparison, the first term of comparison is given by comfort: bathtubs are more comfortable than showers. I'll tell you a secret: this is a false myth, or at least it is today. The so-called Hi-tech showers have the most modern technology and innovations in the world of electronics. These are shower enclosures equipped with comfortable seats and which are really super-equipped, allowing options for hydromassage, Turkish bath, chromo-therapy, aroma-therapy, etc... The only difference with the bathtub? The impossibility of lying down completely, but otherwise a good shower with hi-tech technology has nothing less to offer than a whirlpool tub, indeed perhaps it has some more relaxation functions.

The showers harmonize well with modern and refined furniture design. In fact, many shower stalls are built with transparent glass and the plates are decorated with sophisticated geometric shapes, which give a touch of truly glamorous style to your bathroom.

BATH OR SHOWER, WHY CHOOSE IF YOU CAN OPT FOR THE TUB WITH SHOWER?

Do you believe that having the total comfort of a bathtub combined with the practicality of a shower can only be a pipe dream? You are wrong, as there is the possibility of installing tubs with showers in your bathroom.

If you already have a bathtub and do not want to make excessive expenses to have the convenience of a shower, you can adopt this solution, that is to keep the original bathtub and change only the taps, which will be of the type for shower with shower head.

You can add the tempered glass closure in two doors, one of which is sliding, or completely close the tub by opting for a self-supporting structure, fixed to the wall at the two side ends, with a sliding opening. It is also possible to mount a shower box on the tub with folding and stackable doors which, if not used, leave the tub completely free.

BATHROOM RENOVATION IDEAS

BATHROOM
Remodeling with an Architect

BATHROOM
Remodeling with an Architect

The bathroom of the house, whether it is the master or service, small or large, made of stone, wood or tiles, is a very important environment in our daily life.

 It is the place where we take care of ourselves after a long day and it must be welcoming and functional, so as to allow the simplicity of each operation.

To rediscover harmony and relaxation, aesthetic and functional elements combine with the same importance. Only by achieving the perfect harmony between design, aesthetics and functionality can we obtain the balance that this area of the house needs.

After years of use, the bathroom may need a makeover: there are many ideas for renovating it.

RENOVATING THE BATHROOM: SMALL DETAILS FOR A NEW STYLE

For the restyling of the bathroom, it is not always necessary to carry out renovations. Sometimes, to give new life to an environment, small touches are enough that have the power to give a new flavor to the room. Here are some ideas that will allow you to make your bathroom more modern:

- ❖ Add mirrors and light points;
- ❖ Choose new wallpaper;
- ❖ Install new wall cabinets;
- ❖ Decorate with design objects;

ADD LIGHTS AND MIRRORS.

Often, poorly detailed lighting helps to give the bathroom a melancholy air. In fact, if not well lit, the bathroom can appear more old-fashioned than it really is. For best results, we recommend adding spotlights above the mirror or even a simple dimmable lamp that illuminates the room and makes daily toilet operations easier. To create a play of light and the illusion of a larger bathroom, even a mirror can revolutionize the environment. Installed in the right position, it will create a stunning effect. Seeing is believing!

CHOOSE THE WALLPAPER

If you are tired of tiles, you can also use wallpaper in this environment. An easy solution, to give a completely different look to your bathroom, which can also be applied over the existing covering.

Very fashionable in the last year is the wallpaper with vertical black and white stripes, which goes very well with a retro style but also with a modern black & white bathroom.

INSTALL NEW WALL CABINETS

Clutter and scattered objects can help make the bathroom look scruffy. To avoid this, organize the existing space or, if you have the possibility, add a wall unit. You will immediately see the difference and you will also be facilitated in cleaning operations.

DECORATE WITH DESIGN OBJECTS

To give style to the bathroom you can also add design objects such as knick-knacks. The only rule is not to overdo it: the bathroom must remain tidy and easy to clean. Make your toiletry items stylish: a wooden brush, glam toothbrush and toothpaste containers, a retro shaving set: you can really indulge yourself with ideas!

MODERN BATHROOM: SOME SUGGESTIONS

There are many ideas for renovating a modern bathroom, because this versatile style adapts to the most varied ideas.

One of the most popular in recent seasons is to transform the bathroom into a spa, for moments of pure relaxation. This tip applies to larger bathrooms, which have surfaces large enough to lend themselves to inlays in wood, modern furnishings with essential lines, decorative motifs that recall nature, a stone sink: inspired by luxury spas for your bathroom.

Another brilliant idea to modernize the bathroom, making it totally new, is the creation of a box effect.

This effect is achieved by painting in a single color not only the walls, but also the ceiling, the skirting board and the frames. An elegant solution, capable of enhancing the bathroom with originality, especially if you choose a color in stark contrast to that of the shower cabin and furnishing accessories.

If, on the other hand, you prefer essential furniture, you can make the modern bathroom even more minimal by covering the walls behind the bathroom fixtures with large format tiles. They protect the wall and, at the same time, decorate in a sober and characterful way.

RESTYLING OF A SMALL BATHROOM: HOW TO DO IT

A separate discussion should be made for the bathrooms with limited size. So here are some tips for restyling a small bathroom:

- ❖ Suspended furniture and sanitary ware;
- ❖ Shelves and mirrors with integrated lighting;
- ❖ Shelves built into the wall.

If you want to restore your bathroom, large or small, choose suspended sanitary ware. At the same time, they allow you to save precious space, facilitate bathroom cleaning operations and make the environment appear larger.

If you want to add just a touch of style and make the bathroom tidier, consider a suspended vanity unit instead of one on the ground to give more harmony to the space.

Shelves and mirror with integrated lighting

If you have a small bathroom, think about replacing chandeliers and instead opt for spotlights, mirrors and shelves with integrated lighting. You will achieve the dual purpose of saving space and giving a modern touch to the bathroom.

Shelves built into the wall

Another original idea is to obtain shelves built into the wall. This requires masonry work, so it is only recommended if you are designing the bathroom from scratch or renovating it. In this way, real shelves are created that do not take up extra space in the room but are very useful for storing various toilet items.

REVOLUTIONIZE THE BATHROOM WITH THE PLAY OF LIGHT

Positioning the lights for the bathroom is essential because, in this environment, we find ourselves carrying out activities that require good lighting.

Light is also a piece of furniture with which you can play to further customize the look of our bathroom. The tub area is the one that best lends itself to creativity and imagination. Here are some tips:

It is preferable to place soft lights, preferably of adjustable intensity, to create an atmosphere of true relaxation.

You can decide to emphasize certain areas in particular such as the shower area or the tub area.

You can also opt for scenographic and emotional lighting, perhaps focusing on a "chromotherapy" effect with the use of RGB resistant to water humidity.

One trick is to add mirrors that reflect both the natural light coming from the window and the light points in the bathroom. The environment will immediately seem larger.

So, indulge yourself with mirrors (also backlit), spotlights, a shower with emotional light and lamps: the watchword is to illuminate with style.

COMPLETE RENOVATION: CHANGE THE ARRANGEMENT OF THE FURNITURE

When a small touch-up is not enough, it is advisable to evaluate a real bathroom renovation, which will be more or less profound depending on the conditions of wear of the space and personal needs.

Before any initiative, it is important to have in mind the goal you want to achieve and the style you are looking for. For example, if yours is an outdated bathroom, let's consider a modern renovation that adapts to the rest of the house.

Evaluate wood, an elegant and modern material, lighting it with sanitary fixtures with an essential profile. Choose geometric shapes and choose a transparent glass shower enclosure, which will immediately give a new look to the bathroom.

CLADDING HEIGHT

The covering of the walls and floor of the bathroom is one of the first things to choose when starting to furnish this room of the house: a choice that has undergone several changes over time both with respect to the aesthetics of the surface and the installation methods.

In the past, the laying height of the tile varied from 1.2 to 1.5 meters from the ground up to the middle of the wall, leaving the upper section uncovered, which remained white.

An alternative to this solution today consists in creating the cladding up to the height of the door, that is from 2 to 2.2 meters, thus allowing to be less constrained on the design of the tile, choosing to insert different color or surface divisions to obtain dynamic and unique patterns. The uncovered part is therefore only in the conjunction with the ceiling, to be refreshed from time to time.

In recent years, bathroom cladding has instead preferred a more contemporary and practical solution, applying the tiles up to the ceiling, reaching a height of 2.70 meters, obviously except for lowered ceilings with plasterboard. The look in this case is pleasant and elegant: the vertical parts are made compact, linearity triumphs, the non-evidentness of the joints, thanks for example to the laying of large format tiles such as laminated porcelain stoneware slabs, 100 x 300 cm.

Apart from the painting of the ceiling, the need for periodic whitewashing is therefore eliminated and the walls are completely protected from dirt, mold and humidity. Today's innovation has also enabled the creation of antibacterial plates.

The aesthetics of the surfaces has instead shifted towards a dual chromatic choice: on the one hand the preference for neutral shades that are highly appreciated because they favor the relaxation and intimacy of the bathroom and on the other decorative solutions that give character and personality to space. Full-wall coverings, in the name of functionality and aesthetic refinement, represent the latest trend for bathroom coverings, available in different styles, colors and surfaces to satisfy every design requirement.

The bathroom is, together with the kitchen, one of the most lived-in rooms in the house: between splashes, showers and humidity, the cleaning of the walls is at risk. For this reason, its walls must be protected with a special coating, usually tiles.

When it comes to cladding, the question we ask ourselves most frequently is: what is the ideal height? The right choice is the one that allows us to obtain a good result from an aesthetic point of view but also and above all functional.

THE BATHROOM COVERING: THE CHOICE OF MATERIAL

The material used for the wall covering must be waterproof and resistant, capable of removing humidity, splashes and stains of all kinds. For this purpose, wooden slabs, tiles or small stones can be used to create a mosaic bathroom cladding. The aesthetic choices are so many!

Wood

Wood is rarely used as it is more difficult to manage. Before its application it must be treated to make it waterproof. It is chosen especially for the bathrooms with a vintage and Provençale look. The wood can be tinted with pastel colors.

Wood can also have a natural color to give more warmth and familiarity to the bathroom, but also refinement and elegance. In many cases it is also used in combination with parquet to give continuity with the color of the floor.

Ceramic

The most used wall tiles in bathrooms are ceramic tiles. They are coated, in turn, with a special waterproof enamel, from which dirt can be easily removed. This type of coating applied to bathroom tiles manages to prevent the appearance of mold stains on the walls, and ceramic tiles are also very easy to clean: after a shower, splashes can be removed simply with a damp cloth. They are resistant to sudden changes in temperature, time and humidity.

Glass

Another type of coating is glass, which is usually rendered with a colored mosaic that embellishes the bathroom giving a beautiful luminous aesthetic effect. This material can be used in conjunction with other types of liner to add volume and change.

BATHROOM CLADDING: WHAT HEIGHT?

The bathroom cladding, regardless of the material used, can have different heights: it can occupy the entire wall or reach up to 2 meters or 1.20 meters. These are the three most used types of cladding.

In the first case, the cladding covers the entire wall leaving only the ceiling exposed. This solution is the most traditional, it characterizes the bathrooms of the past, but it can be revisited in a modern way: in fact, today the market offers many products to customize the covering. With this choice you get a beautiful and protected wall.

The second very common solution is to apply bathroom tiles up to 2 meters, over the entire surface of the bathroom. In this case the coating reaches up to the door and still guarantees good protection.

You could also opt for a covering divided according to the area's most at risk, namely those in correspondence with the sanitary ware: such as the shower or the sink, always reaching about 2 meters. In this way, even the condensation that tends to rise slightly rests on the tiles without damaging the wall.

Zoned bathroom cladding with tiles

A third option, which has been trendy in recent years, is to create a cladding with a minimum height, which reaches 1.20 meters. This option is the most dangerous even if very fashionable: you risk staining the wall, not only for splashes but also for humidity and condensation, causing ugly mold or fungus stains that are difficult to remove.

We advise you to opt for a high bathroom wall covering that protects the natural color of the wall from dirt.

DECORATING THE CEILING

Sometimes, to renovate the bathroom it is not necessary to resort to precious coverings: just follow some useful tips to give a new look to the house! Colors, lights, plasterboard, polystyrene frames, plaster panels and decorations can be of great help in this regard. Let's find out together how to decorate the ceiling for the bathroom.

One of the most common mistakes is to associate the beauty of a home with a huge expenditure of money. Instead, you can radically improve the look of the rooms, simply by using paints, stencils, panels and frames. Let's start with the first solution: if you have already chosen to decorate the floor with stencils, you can use the same ornamental motif on the ceiling. Flowers and leaves are ideal for those who love the most romantic style; abstract motifs fit perfectly into the modern decorated ceiling; other doodles allow you to decorate the minimal chic apartment with style. In ancient houses you can dare with frescoes and acrylic drawings that reproduce balustrades and subjects inspired by nature, the perfect decorations for Art Nouveau ceilings.

To decorate the bathroom ceiling with paints, we suggest you use natural sponges to create a delicate gradient effect. Choose colors that recall those of the furniture or contrast without exaggerating with vibrant shades such as red or electric blue. The sponging technique is especially indicated for the ceiling of the Turkish bath and in cases where it is necessary to cover very large surfaces: it is preferable to perform it, however, after having repainted the wall with a neutral color.

Another solution for the bathroom ceiling is to apply decorative panels: it is a technique that works well especially in modern-style houses but should be avoided for houses with sloping roofs. In this case, to respect the rustic look of the building, fake beams can be applied to the ceiling, to be painted in the same shade as the walls or left in the natural color of the wood. Finally, a method to enhance the bathroom is to create elegant plays of light: just create a false ceiling and arrange the recessed spotlights to your liking.

HOW TO REMOVE MOLD FROM THE BATHROOM

Mold develops mostly in the bathroom due to the presence of water.

Fortunately, you can easily get rid of it by using simple household cleaning products! Address this by making a vinegar, borax, or bleach solution in a spray bottle. You just spray it in the shower, in the bath, the sink, on the tiles, the joints or mastic. Then use a cloth or toothbrush to remove any mold. You can also remove it from the ceiling and walls using similar methods. When cleaning, always wear protective gloves and ventilate the room.

METHOD 1 PREPARE A SOLUTION TO REMOVE MOLD

1

Create a vinegar-based solution to eliminate mold safely and non-toxic. White vinegar is an excellent remedy for removing mold from different types of surfaces. Pour it directly into a spray bottle and don't dilute it if you don't want to decrease its effectiveness. You don't even have to rinse after use.

While the smell can be unpleasant, it usually goes away within 1-2 hours. You can open a window or turn on the fan if you want to disperse it faster.

Insider Tip: If you need to treat a rather large area or if you don't want to smell the pungent smell of vinegar in the bathroom, you can dilute it by mixing 1 part with 2 parts waters. In this way you will get a larger dose and reduce the odor while leaving the antifungal action of the solution unaltered!

2

Use a borax solution to naturally remove mold. Borax is a natural insecticidal and fungicidal substance. Mix 200 g in about 4 liters of water and pour the solution into a spray bottle. Just spray it directly on the surface to be cleaned. There is no need to rinse because borax is able to inhibit the return of mold.

You can find borax in the detergent aisle at the supermarket. It is a white chalky powder.

It is dangerous to ingest, but unlike bleach it does not produce toxic fumes.

3

Opt for a bleach solution as a last resort. Although bleach is effective in removing mold from non-porous surfaces, such as showers, sinks and tiles, it is a toxic substance that must be used with care. Make a solution of 1 part bleach and 10 parts water and pour it into a spray bottle. It should not be rinsed unless there is a risk that pets or small children will come into contact with the treated area.

Always wear gloves when handling this substance and circulate air to avoid inhaling the fumes.

Bleach can cause irritation to eyes, lungs and skin.

METHOD 2 USE A CLEANSING SOLUTION

1

Spray the anti-mold cleaner on the area to be cleaned. Get a vaporizer containing the solution you want to use. Spray it generously over the entire area to form a visible, even layer. Avoid completely impregnating the surface, otherwise you will later be forced to remove the excess liquid. Try to apply enough so as to visibly moisten the area to be treated, but not too much so that you can make patches of detergent.

Be very careful not to slip when treating tiles or grout.

2

Wipe smooth surfaces with a cloth to remove mold. Fold it in four parts and wipe it all over the area where you sprayed the cleaning solution. The mold should adhere easily. Switch sides each time the previous one gets dirty or soaked in residue.

You will probably have to change it and use another one especially if you need to clean a large area.

Alternatively, if you prefer, you can use a sponge instead of the cloth.

By smooth surfaces we mean those of the shower, bathtub, sink and tiles.

3

Use a brush to remove stubborn mold from smooth surfaces. If the mold doesn't go away, switch to the hard way! Rub the affected area vigorously until it comes off. Afterward, try to get rid of any newly formed traces so you don't have to scrub.

Keep a brush to use specifically for mold in the bathroom to prevent the spores from spreading to the rest of the house.

4

Use a toothbrush on tile joints or putty. Remove mold from joints or putty with an old toothbrush. Move it back and forth. As you go, rinse it under running water to remove any mold and prevent spores from spreading throughout the bathroom.

Keep a toothbrush to use specifically for mold in the bathroom to prevent the spores from spreading throughout your home.

You can use a larger brush if you prefer, but a toothbrush is easier to use in tight spaces.

You can purchase a grout brush at home improvement stores.

5

Dry the treated area with a cloth. Remove excess liquid from the area you just cleaned to keep the bathroom dry and avoid slipping. Wipe the cloth over all smooth surfaces, joints or putty to absorb excess moisture. By doing this, you can also remove all the mold residues that came off when you brushed with the toothbrush.

You may want to change the cloth if it gets too wet.

Watch out for crevices and corners to prevent moisture from building up and other mold forming.

6

Add some grout or putty if you can't get rid of the stains. If too much mold has built up, you won't be able to remove it. In this case, you can use a flat-blade screwdriver to dig into the interstices and try to remove the traces of mold. Fill with more grout or putty and clean the treated area regularly to avoid it becoming moldy again.

You can apply a sealant material to the grout or putty to prevent other stains from forming.

METHOD 3 PREVENT MOLD IN THE BATHROOM

1

Turn on the ventilator when taking a bath or shower. This allows you to reduce the humidity in the bathroom. Turn it on when you start taking a bath or shower and let it run for at least another 5 minutes after you're done to disperse the steam. If you can, try keeping it on until the steam disappears completely.

To dissipate moisture faster, open the window and turn on the ventilator.

2

Open the window after you have taken a bath or shower. Mold forms faster when the humidity rises, for example when washing. Open the window immediately after taking a bath or shower to evaporate any traces of water and disperse excess steam. Keep it open until the bathroom dries.

Remember to open it immediately after a shower to limit mold growth.

3

Dry all surfaces if you are concerned that the humidity inside is high. While regular cleaning and air circulation should keep mold at bay, sometimes these precautions aren't enough. If you find a spot where mold continues to form, wipe it off every time you use water in the bathroom.

The areas where it tends to develop the most are the sink or shower tiles.

Instead of the cloth you can use a squeegee on the tiles and on the glass of the doors.

METHOD 4 ADOPT SECURITY MEASURES

1

Use rubber gloves when applying anti-mold treatments. Avoid touching it with your bare hands. If you use vinegar or borax, a normal pair of rubber gloves for household use is sufficient. However, if you handle bleach, opt for those made of natural rubber or PVC.

Remove them as soon as you're done cleaning so the spores don't spread throughout the house.

2

Wear old clothes and wash them with hot water. It is preferable to put on old clothes because they can be stained or damaged in contact with the cleaning solutions and hot water of the laundry in the washing machine. Always wash them at high temperatures as soon as you have finished cleaning the mold to kill the spores trapped in the fabric and prevent them from spreading.

This advice is especially true if you use bleach, as it can discolor fabrics.

3

Circulate the air while cleaning. Open as many windows as possible and, if possible, turn on the ventilator. These measures will prevent you from inhaling the spores and any toxic fumes that may be released during the use of detergents.

You can also keep a portable fan in the bathroom.

Warnings

If someone in the house is allergic to mold or has compromised immune systems, it is best for them to go out while you are cleaning the bathroom to prevent them from inhaling the spores.

Contact a cleaning company if you are unable to remove mold on your own, have health problems caused by the presence of mold, or if the area to be treated is larger than 1 m².

TIPS TO PREVENT MOLD IN THE BATHROOM

How many times have you found yourself struggling with mold in the bathroom, present on the corners of the walls or inside the joints of the shower tray or tiles?

Have you thought and thought about the causes of this annoying inconvenience, but have not been able to come to a conclusion? In reality, black mold in the bathroom is a rather common but not at all healthy phenomenon, which needs to be removed in order to avoid damage to your bathroom. So, let's see some tips on how to fight mold and how to prevent its formation.

MOLD IN THE BATHROOM: WHAT IS IT AND WHAT ARE THE CAUSES OF ITS FORMATION?

Mold in the bathroom is a very frequent phenomenon due to the proliferation of spores due to poor air circulation. In addition to being more frequent in closed environments, however, it is important to know that the growth of mold is due to the presence of humidity and condensation in the air on which the spores feed.

It is therefore easy to understand that the bathroom is one of the rooms most exposed to this phenomenon precisely because it is the place where condensation is easiest to form. During an invigorating shower or hot bath, for example, the formation of steam is more than natural. To avoid, however, that it gives rise to condensation, it is advisable to properly dry each surface while cleaning the bathroom and take care of the correct air exchange in the environment. For this reason, the sooner you understand why mold forms on bathroom walls, the sooner it will be possible to root out the problem.

In fact, water vapor condensation is not the only cause of mold growth in the bathroom. Even the use of washable paints - not recommended for humid environments such as the bathroom - or an excessive thermal shock between the internal and external temperature could favor the formation of mold. So let's see how to prevent and how to permanently eliminate mold from the bathroom.

How to prevent mold from forming in the bathroom?

There are some measures you can follow to prevent the formation of mold in the bathroom or on the surfaces, for example, of the

BATHROOM
Remodeling with an Architect

shower tray or pipes. In fact, it is important to know that mold proliferates on any type of surface, whether it be walls or even bathroom fixtures. The most common place, however, remain the walls and it is therefore important to take small precautions to prevent the formation of mold on the ceiling or on the surfaces of the bathroom, such as:

- ❖ often whitewash the walls of the bathroom and avoid the use of paints containing gypsum, as they are more predisposed to retain humidity and, therefore, more vulnerable to the formation of mold;
- ❖ use tiles near washbasins, bathtubs and shower stalls, to avoid direct contact between water and walls;
- ❖ adequately warm the bathroom before using it for personal hygiene. In fact, the colder the bathroom, the more the steam from the water will create condensation which, in the long run, will inevitably lead to the formation of mold in the bathroom.

Therefore, mold in the bathroom is a common problem, which requires small operations to be controlled and eradicated. In fact, with a few tricks and the right remedies, mold in the shower or on the ceiling will be just a bad memory.

NATURAL REMEDIES FOR MOLD

One of the problems that plagues many houses and apartments is the deposit of mold. We are talking about a multicellular fungus that finds fertile ground in indoor places, characterized by a

116 | P a g .

particularly high degree of humidity. So, what does it look like? And what dangers can it entail?

Mold mainly forms on the walls of a house and its downsides are not limited to its anti-aesthetic presence. It is recommended to remove it quickly, as it can potentially cause health problems, as well as damage to the walls.

So how can the presence of this harmful fungus be recognized? First of all, mold makes itself felt due to its very unpleasant smell capable of dispersing numerous toxins into the atmosphere. All this can become a risk for asthmatic and allergic subjects, since it affects the lungs in the first place. Even after eliminating the mold, its smell can remain inside the house but, fortunately, it can be easily eliminated.

As for the walls, mold manifests itself with its typical black-greenish color. But it can also settle between bathroom tiles, in the shower and even in cupboards and drawers. It is therefore necessary to try to eliminate it immediately and it is possible to do so thanks to some very simple methods.

Here are the best natural remedies to get rid of mold and its smell from your home:

1) Air exchange

First of all, to prevent the formation of mold, the first advice is to make sure that your home is often subject to a change of air, even for a few minutes a day. The apartment should remain at a constant and average temperature, while when it rains the window should be left closed. Another method to prevent it from forming is to leave a small gap between the furniture and the wall, one or 2 centimeters is enough, while rooms with high humidity should not be furnished with carpet. These are preventive measures, if instead you need to eradicate the mold already present on your walls, let's see what to use and how.

2) If you don't want to use bleach

Here's how to make a particular solution with water, hydrogen peroxide, bicarbonate and fine salt. Here is the recipe in more detail:

Ingredients:

- 700 ml of water
- 2 tablespoons of 30/40 vol. hydrogen peroxide.
- 2 tablespoons of baking soda
- 2 tablespoons of fine salt.

Dissolve bicarbonate and salt up into the water, in a spray bottle of at least one liter of capacity. Add the hydrogen peroxide and mix the bottle well before using it. After spraying on the area affected by mold, rub it with an abrasive cloth, or rather, with an upholstery brush or an old toothbrush. The result will surprise you. No more mold around the house!

3) Lavender remedy

For this anti-mold solution, you need: 100 ml of denatured alcohol and lavender essential oil. Just add 1 drop of essential oil to the alcohol to get a powerful ally against green stains on the walls. Mix the two liquids in a spray bottle, shake it firmly and spray the contents on the mold: then let it act for a few minutes and remove the residues with an old (but clean) brush.

4) Grapefruit remedy

The ingredients in this case are: water with the addition of two effective anti-fungal agents, namely grapefruit extract and Tea Tree essential oil. Mix 500 ml of water with 2 teaspoons of grapefruit extract and 2 teaspoons of Tea Tree essential oil: spray everything on the contaminated area and let it rest. Finally, wipe with a clean, damp cloth. Finally open the window and let it air for at least 8 hours.

5) Cinnamon remedy

With this recipe you will get not only an anti-mold solution but also a fragrant home deodorant! For the preparation you will need 15 drops of cinnamon essential oil, 10 drops of manuka essential oil (very similar to Tea Tree Oil), 200 ml of water and 200 ml of apple cider vinegar. Mix all the ingredients and, as always, spray the resulting solution onto the stain. In addition to eliminating mold, you will smell a pleasant cinnamon scent in its place!

6) Remedy with water and white vinegar

An excellent natural remedy to eliminate mold not only from the home but also from cabinets or drawers is represented by a solution of water and white vinegar. Prepare a basin in which you will pour 3 cups of water and 3 cups of white vinegar. Add a few drops of juniper essential oil and a little cinnamon. Mix and pour the solution into a spray bottle, like those used at the sea to get wet while sunbathing on the beach. Spray the solution directly on the mold and then rub with a cloth dampened with warm water until the stains are gone. Then air the room for at least 8-9 hours by keeping the cabinet doors and drawers open if you have eliminated mold from these places.

7) Remedy with vinegar and hydrogen peroxide against the most persistent mold

A solution based on vinegar and hydrogen peroxide is a really effective method against the most persistent mold, especially against that deposited between the tiles or in the shower. Then dilute the vinegar with the hydrogen peroxide in a medium-sized bowl. After mixing, pour the contents into a spray bottle and spray directly on the mold deposits in your shower.

This way, the bacteria will be affected immediately. Then, with an old toothbrush, scrape between the tiles or mold deposits in the shower. If, on the other hand, mold is on the walls, a cloth moistened with warm water will be needed to eliminate the mold. Remember not to neglect the most difficult to reach corners and rinse with warm water. As always, once everything is finished, the advice is always to let it air for at least 8 hours.

8) Steam as a remedy for mold

Among the remedies we propose, this is the only one that involves the use of an appliance capable of producing steam under pressure. So, if you have one, spray the steam on the area where mold is present. Be meticulous and, using a mask, concentrate on the most difficult areas, such as tile joints, where the dirt is most stubborn. Repeat the operation until the joint is completely clean. Finally, proceed to rinse the treated surface with water. In this way all dirt residues will be permanently eliminated.

9) Eliminate the smell of mold and humidity

The smell of damp and mold can occur, as well as on clothes that may have been in closets or drawers where it was present, even in the rooms where it has been eliminated. There are also numerous natural remedies to solve this problem, so it is not necessary to buy who knows which room fragrances or use sprays that have the same purpose.

10) Milk against the smell of mold and humidity

This is a real grandmother's remedy. A cup of boiling milk could solve the musty odor problem in drawers and cabinets. Leave it on a shelf of your wardrobe, or inside a drawer, for about 12 hours, taking care to close the doors and drawers. Next, open and let the air circulate freely. The milk will have absorbed the bad smell. But this is not the only natural remedy for the smell of mold and humidity, as we will see in the next point.

11) Lavender against the smell of mold

If you prefer to rely on a perfumed solution, you can make it yourself: if you love lavender, just dry a few twigs and put them in a perforated bag. This, left in the room, or in the closet, or in the drawers from which you have eliminated the mold, will release its scent immediately. Lemon can also be useful for this purpose.

12) Lemon zest against the musty smell

Lemon zest can also be very useful against the smell of mold and humidity. The recommendation is to scrape it off the lemon in order to leave fairly large strips of peel. Then, it is placed in a basin filled with 1/4 of lemon juice and 3/4 of very hot water. The dimensions of the basin must be proportional to the size of the room. If you have to put it in cabinets and drawers, a glass will suffice. Finally, it is left in the room for at least a couple of days to allow the smell to spread. If it is winter, you can instead leave the lemon zest directly on hot radiators.

If mold stains have appeared on the bathroom walls, remember to ventilate more often and solve the problem by choosing one of these natural measures.

BATHROOM
Remodeling with an Architect

The bathroom, as we know, is an environment that easily suffers damage due to humidity, especially if it is not adequately ventilated. It is always helpful, therefore, to know what to do when those ugly mold stains appear on the bathroom ceiling.

The techniques are different, but as you may have guessed, the first step is to ensure proper ventilation. Sometimes, however, it is not easy, since the bathroom does not always have large windows like the rest of the house.

Another elementary tip is to make sure that there is no water infiltration in the wall. In this case, the mold stains on the bathroom ceiling could appear within a few days.

Finally, to prevent the formation of mold on the walls, the installation of a good thermal insulator, optimal lighting - preferably natural - and evaluating the arrangement of a dehumidifier or a humidity extractor are ideal.

ANOTHER METHOD IS TO USE TEA TREE OIL.

It is one of the most powerful natural disinfectants in existence. By preparing a simple solution with this ingredient, you can quickly get rid of mold.

Ingredients

- 2 tablespoons of tea tree oil (30 ml)
- 2 cups of water (500 ml)

How to proceed?

Hand spray mildew cleaner on the bathroom ceiling.

With the help of a nebulizer and, of course, wearing gloves, spray this solution on the stains.

In a few minutes they will begin to lighten; after rinsing, the wall will be ready for a good painting; first make sure that the humidity is not caused by water infiltration.

HOW TO CHOOSE A BATHROOM FLOOR

W hat types of tiles are suitable for the bathroom? How to proceed with their installation?

Ceramic tiles, masonry tiles, as well as parquet and the newcomer, cork, are all materials that compete for the primacy for the covering of the walls and floors of the entire house. However, everyone has their own sector, therefore, it is essential to know the field of application of each coating and then choose the one that seems best suited to the needs and preferences.

Usually for the covering of damp environments, such as bathrooms and kitchens, tiles hold the primacy, although lately, parquet (and to a lesser extent cork), is entering this new field of application. New technologies and new materials studies provide new support for construction.

Therefore, tiles are still the favorites when it comes to covering the bathroom, since their characteristics make them extremely resistant.

WHAT ARE THE FEATURES THAT A TILE MUST HAVE TO BE SUITABLE FOR THE BATHROOM?

The bathroom is, together with the kitchen, the wettest place in a house and this factor could ruin its appearance and functionality. The bathroom is also one of the places in which the family shares various moments, therefore the covering must guarantee, in addition to a defense against possible bacterial attacks, also a high level of hygiene.

Choosing a product for the bathroom coating, therefore, consists in an act of respect for your home and for your personal hygiene. The materials to be used for the bathroom must not absorb water (or in any case must guarantee absorption in minimal quantities), they must have a particular chemical composition, so as not to allow cleaning products to affect their consistency. In addition, the materials used for the bathroom lining must be easy to clean and very resistant.

The material par excellence to be used in the bathroom would be natural stone, but ceramic, stoneware or terracotta tiles are also widely used and certainly guarantee a much lower cost.

WHAT ARE THE MAIN TYPES OF TILES SUITABLE FOR THE BATHROOM?

Before buying bathroom wall tiles, it is necessary to know the different types on the market, in order not to remain helpless in the face of the many varieties and not be able to choose correctly.

For bathroom cladding, specialist retailers offer a range of choice that varies between the following types:

- single-fired tiles, characterized by a glazed surface, formed by pressing with a unique cooking process, which involves the support and the glaze simultaneously; they are used above all for the internal flooring of bathrooms and rarely for external environments, since they do not guarantee a high resistance to continuous and constant water flows;
- double-fired tiles are produced by means of a double cooking, the first for the support, the second for the enamel and are characterized by a shiny surface but at the same time delicate, precisely for this reason, they are little used for the construction of pavements, but largely for coatings;
- the white-body (known for its high quality) and pink-body tiles are two variants of the double-fired tiles;
- maiolica tiles constitute a typically Italian product and are used for lining the internal walls of the bathroom, since

they ensure good mechanical strength. With porosity ranging from 10% to 25%; they are unsuitable for flooring;

- red stoneware tiles are not glazed and are characterized by a compact red support; they are formed by pressing; nowadays this type of tile is not widely used;
- porcelain stoneware tiles are characterized by a clear or colored support and are obtained by pressing; their resistance and high porosity, as well as their technical characteristics, have marked their wide diffusion and their use in many fields; porcelain stoneware tiles can be glazed or have a natural surface, they can be colored in the mass or have a non-colored support; they can be subjected to different treatments, including polishing or lapping, according to the aesthetic result that is desired;
- terracotta tiles are produced by extrusion and are characterized by red support, and the porous surface is not glazed;
- three- and four-fired tiles are made with layered decorations and therefore three or four firings with progressively lower temperatures are indispensable.

HOW IS THE INSTALLATION OF THE BATHROOM TILES CARRIED OUT?

Before carrying out the actual laying of the tiles inside the bathroom, it is necessary to plan and carefully evaluate which parts must be totally covered, which will constitute the most visible areas, in order to know how to proceed and avoid any imperfections stand out to the eye, especially if you proceed by means of a DIY technique.

An essential step before laying the tiles is choosing the size and quantity to buy. The smaller the tiles, the easier they can be handled, in order to hide some inaccuracies.

There are different ways to know the exact quantity of tiles to buy, but looking on the web, you can come across a practical, fast and automatic method, which allows you to accurately calculate the exact number of elements needed. It is a program that allows you to create an electronic spreadsheet, essentially an alternative method to design your own bathroom.

For the coating of a bathroom, you will need the following tools:

- a ruler and a pencil;
- a drill;
- a square;
- a hacksaw;
- a level;
- the glue;
- any self-leveling product;
- the tiles.

We proceed with the actual laying of the bathroom tiles, deciding from which precise point to start. Usually, the whole tiles, that is, those with the edges, should cover the entire spaces, while, gradually, the tiles will be cut when you get closer to the corners.

BATHROOM
Remodeling with an Architect

In general, it is advisable to start from the end of the door, taking care to space the tiles. It is necessary to proceed with the laying of the tiles following a single row and then continue in the opposite direction.

The tiles can be positioned following decorations diagonally, running, or according to customized designs, moreover, they can be placed flush, with no space between one and the other, or spaced by means of a joint.

When laying the tiles in the bathroom it is necessary to consider the possible presence of holes for the pipes or cables, which will be surrounded by well-cut tiles according to the precise shape.

By means of a spirit level, always check the regularity of the flooring. Proceed with cutting the irregular elements with the appropriate hacksaw.

The glue must be applied with a notched trowel directly onto the wall, if the room to be covered is large, taking care not to occupy a very high surface, otherwise the glue would risk drying; if the bathroom is small, you can also opt for applying glue directly to the back of the tiles.

It is necessary to allow 24 hours to pass and then spread the joint filler over the entire surface.

It is necessary to cover the edges of the sink, tub and shower tray with the special anti-mold silicone sealant, in order to avoid dark halos, or annoying and harmful water infiltrations.

HOW TO MATCH THE TILES IN THE BATHROOM?

When you think of bathroom tiles, usually classic decors come to mind, if not standardized and monotonous colors. In reality, in our days, continuous research and studies regarding tiles for wet environments have given life to decorations that are increasingly fashionable and in step with the times, able to follow all tastes, trends and styles even the most modern and contemporary ones.

In fact, it is not certain that small tiles are suitable for small bathrooms and large ones for larger rooms. The maintenance of the joints is perhaps the one that requires more work, since it is precisely in these places that molds or bacteria can lurk: elbow grease, steam or specific products can easily restore the joints and tiles as new.

Nowadays, moreover, there are numerous expedients on the market to embellish the bathroom, such as, for example, decorative strips or inserts, which on the one hand can be very expensive, on the other hand they contribute to making the bathroom much more refined and aesthetically pleasing.

Usually, in the presence of a particularly small bathroom, it is necessary to lay light-colored tiles, as we know, in fact, that dark colors tend to darken and restrict the rooms, therefore opting for a light-colored coating will help to give to the bathroom a particular atmosphere, at the same time elegant, airy and harmonious. It is advisable to complete the whole with a large mirror, in order to increase the depth of the small bathroom.

To create a mosaic inside a bathroom, one of the following types of building materials is usually used, namely:

- pebbles;
- glass paste;
- sandstone squares;
- glazed ceramic;
- marble;
- specific bathroom tiles;
- glass enamels.

BATHROOM STYLES

Whether it is created in a narrow environment, or a real room is reserved, the bathroom is confirmed as one of the most refined and refined areas of an apartment. Here are the styles for the furniture.

COUNTRY CHIC

Regardless of the size available, the country chic style is an option that can adapt to any type of bathroom. Especially for a house outside the city, perhaps in the countryside, recalling rustic details but always with elegant finishes.

The materials used by those who opt for this solution are ceramic and wood (especially for furnishings and decorations). But the game of balance halfway between rustic and refined is also suitable for the bathrooms of city apartments.

CONTEMPORARY STYLE

Essential and elegant but never gaunt. The contemporary style perfectly blends a minimal taste with other more refined ones (above all the industrial one). This solution is particularly suitable for bathrooms that lack a little brightness and small ones, in which it manages to mask the dimensions in the best possible way, enhancing the quality of the materials and the creativity of the design that focuses on the shiny and clear space.

SCANDINAVIAN STYLE

This option, on the other hand, is for those who want to give liveliness to the style of their bathroom. Its main features are light tones and wood. In the Scandinavian style, white is very present, which makes it perfect for giving regularity to environments with particularly articulated heights and plants (in attics and under the roof).

VINTAGE STYLE

The personal touch should be carefully measured when you try your hand at vintage style, which is already a must in the other rooms of the house but is also increasingly appreciated for bathroom furnishings. There are few standard lines, but accumulating too many elements that recall the past could be counterproductive.

The ideal would be to include a maximum of a couple of antiques (or, perhaps better still, modern antiques). A mirror or a washbasin stand could make the difference.

CLASSIC STYLE

Timeless and always trendy. A bathroom furnished in a classic style, perhaps with some modern reinterpretation, is always the right answer. Marble and wood are the leitmotif that guarantee visual impact, but it is also characterized by the breadth of bathroom fixtures and washbasins that recall vaguely retro lines and taps with an absolutely minimalist design.

ROMANTIC STYLE

A dip into a bygone era, the romantic style is the perfect option for those who want to amaze with an unsettling bathroom furniture solution. It recalls a bohemian atmosphere and is characterized by inevitable details such as bucolic wallpaper (often referring to themes of leaves and flowers), washbasins and sanitary ware with neoclassical lines, mirrors with gold finishes and an inevitable free-standing bathtub on lion claw feet

INDUSTRIAL STYLE

"Rough" surfaces, concrete walls and intense colors. The industrial style, one of the most followed trends for home furnishings in recent years, has also arrived in bathrooms. The basic materials are metal and raw wood, as well as recycled materials and the inevitable stoneware slabs and white tiles. It is particularly suitable for a second bathroom.

ZEN STYLE

Building a corner of the Orient in the bathroom. Here is the Zen style, an exaltation of essential elegance and a place of pleasure and relaxation par excellence. They are perfectly designed to be balanced and essential, without skimping on the aesthetic aspect. They blend natural elements such as wood in bathtubs that use hi- tech taps.

ORIENTAL STYLE

The oriental style also winks at the Rising Sun, reminiscent of the typical Asian spas. Basically, it is an ethnic matrix, which recalls a timeless era to enhance well-being and harmony, all thanks to the choice of essential decorative elements and colors with soft shades and strong tones such as blue and red.

LIBERTY STYLE

Typical of the early twentieth century, the liberty style is synonymous with elegance. And, even in the bathroom, it knows how to give a touch of sober refinement. Composed of elements characterizing small sinks with double taps, floors and walls made with small and often diamond-cut tiles. It represents the ideal solution for a large bathroom, in which to insert decorations and boiserie on the walls typical of those years.

DARK STYLE

More and more trendy. The choice of black for the bathroom is conquering large slices of the market. And often mixing the intensity of this color with some white details can represent the right solution to create an alchemy on which to play to mix the styles as well. It is particularly suitable for traditional materials such as wood and ceramic.

THE BATHROOM IN BLACK AND WHITE

Classic and always trendy, the black / white combination is able to transform a small and narrow room into an elegant and particular environment. With the right furnishings and studied color shades, even the beloved black & white becomes a choice of character.

OPTICAL FANTASIES

Do you love vintage but don't want to give up elegance? Black and white is the right idea to decorate your small bathroom.

Cover the walls with black and white striped wallpaper: vertical and thick are better, and your room will appear larger. Create continuity with the flooring: choose a dark and shiny material, natural stones are a great idea.

BATHROOM
Remodeling with an Architect

To add depth to the room, you can cover only the upper part of the walls with striped wallpaper and choose a dark solid color covering from the floor to the height of the sink and the bathroom fixtures. Enhance the detachment by creating profiles (also in plasterboard) in white. You can also use this idea to create fake frames that help enliven the room.

If you want to make the bathroom more precious, choose decorations and details in gold color. There are also taps in this shade! And to give character to the environment, hang a stylish mirror, and if you are not afraid to dare, choose a frame in the French style: it seems to come out of the walls.

Complete the decor with an important suspension chandelier, also in gold.

CHIC GRAPHICS

By playing with black and white tiles you can create designs that transform your small bathroom into a très chic room.

Choose tiles with white decorations on a black base, opt for geometric designs, prefer vertical and oblique strokes that lengthen the look and help make your room appear larger. For this reason, it is preferable to choose large format tiles: they have minimal joints, so they give the impression of forming a single surface. The result is very elegant.

You can go up with the tiles up to the middle of the wall to about 120 centimeters and enhance the profile of the covering with a black raised border. To lighten the room, respecting the sense of elegance that characterizes it, cover the remaining part of the wall with a washable black paint.

To make the room brighter, choose a mirror polished steel sink that reflects the chromatic effects of the tiles. A built-in sink on a piece of furniture with sinuous shapes is indicated to reinforce the final result: a small and precious, elegant and chic environment.

CLASS EXPERIMENTS

The black and white contrasts allow you to experiment. Timeless and trendy, with these shades you can be daring, avoiding mistakes (and regrets) that you could easily commit with other colors.

A mirrored wall is the most interesting solution to choose if you want to expand the size of your bathroom. To make it more of character, enhance it with a profile (10 to 15 centimeters high to make it important) of dark color. Combine a monobloc floor-mounted washbasin: for a result of great aesthetic impact, choose the model with the drain in the floor. You will need a plumbing intervention: take advantage of it, and ask to make a faucet in style as well. Create a color harmony with black.

Illuminate the environment by creating a play of movement by hanging suspended lights, always black, at different heights. LED spotlights are preferred because they help to give personality to the room. Towel racks hanging on the side of the central area of the bathroom complete the setting, almost defining the depth of the space. Decorate the walls with prints and paintings with dark frames, contrasting with the color of the walls. In this way you will create an environment that is as original as it is fascinating, ideal for the guest bathroom.

REFLECTIONS AND NEW PERSPECTIVES

If you want to add thickness to a long, narrow room, choose a dark coating to apply to the walls. You can hang a wallpaper that recreates the effect of many small bricks: opt for a black background with light profiles. Tiles, especially if the bathroom is limited in size, will make it appear even smaller. A flooring in shades of gray helps you make the environment brighter and creates a play of shades that lightens the setting, without losing elegance. A tip: place the tiles chosen for the floor at an angle, it will help you broaden the perspective.

Add a round pedestal sink to make the room more harmonious. Complete the decor with a mirror, preferably without a frame for a neater effect. Choose a cabinet with mirrored surfaces to place in a corner of the bathroom to reflect the space and help make it appear larger.

ELEGANT MINIMALISM

If you need a lot lighter in the bathroom, it is advisable to choose white for the walls. Opt for a black sink and choose glossy surfaces: they reflect light and make rooms look more sophisticated.

You can combine black and white with dark gray, but for a more harmonious result avoid other color combinations; and be careful not to combine glossy surfaces with matte tops, even if they are of the same shade.

Round shapes are sweeter and more romantic, unlike the more decisive square lines. You can combine a round countertop washbasin on a square black glass top for a delicate effect. The floor will be the central element of the room. For this, choose a simple mirror and chandelier devoid of personality; recessed spotlights are also indicated.

Steel goes well with shades of white and black. Choose gloss to reinforce the timeless elegance of this play of colors.

SOPHISTICATED LUXURY

A glossy white bidet accompanied by a countertop with built-in washbasin, always in the same shade and style, become the protagonist objects of a context as luxurious as it is eccentric.

You can choose to play with black and white tiles in an infinity of variations. For example, you could cover the walls of the bathroom, from top to bottom, with black rectangular tiles: a combination of shapes will be born where the joints form a subtle design, almost like a gray pencil that seems to have left its mark on the walls. The covering creates the impression of a luxurious box, whose harmony is broken by the mirror: thin and transparent to reflect, and almost amplify, the effect of the room. The result is strong, eclectic and linear.

For the floor you can opt for a large white tile, defined by a black profile that highlights it: the impression is that of a carpet that contrasts the room.

BOISERIE WITH CHARACTER

The color black helps you to make a modern, contemporary boiserie.

Applied to the walls of your bathroom, they transform a small room giving it personality. Unusual and also very particular is its declination in the glossy ceramic version cut in large sizes. Opt for panels with sharply cut edges (and not beveled) so as to combine more elements and enhance the profiles by applying backsplashes.

To embellish the room by enhancing this choice, opt for French-style furnishings and details. You can apply paintings with frames in shades of gold or bronze to the walls. A mirror with side lamps is an interesting piece of furniture.

Suitable for the flooring are black and white ceramic mosaic tiles: create a design that will be the basis of the environment; if you want to make the room brighter and lighter, go for white and use black tiles only to delimit the contours of the space. If, on the other hand, you want to give it more depth, it is better to position them so as to create vertical lines, parallel to the long side of the room, which project the gaze towards the main wall.

QUIRKY CHOICES

Is your bathroom small and are you looking for a simple and high-impact solution? Black and white wallpaper can be the answer to your questions and allows you to impress with style!

Choose one of the many patterns with black and white decorations (floral if you are looking for a romantic style, geometric if you prefer rigor) and apply it on the walls of your room, at full height so as to create a box: the result will be as eccentric as it is elegant.

Place the bathroom fixtures, strictly white to avoid chromatic excesses. Choose the furniture: pursue minimalism, the less the better, so your room doesn't look too heavy. And for the flooring, choose a light color and a simple material such as ceramic.

A black central pendant chandelier with classic and elegant shapes helps to define the boundaries of the space.

LIGHTING

BATHROOM
Remodeling with an Architect

In the search for an ideal solution for bathroom lighting, you must always consider what are two fundamental aspects in a project of this type:

- the importance of light as a piece of furniture;

- the functionality of a customized lighting system.

If you only consider the aesthetic aspect of the lights to be installed in a bathroom, you can choose from a vast assortment of original and refined lighting elements in the style of your choice, from classic, to modern, to vintage. However, to obtain a perfect result it is also necessary to evaluate functionality, adequately arranging the various light points in the bathroom and using, if possible, LED lamps of the right intensity (usually around 60 W).

The game is to identify the perfect balance between designer bathroom lighting and a welcoming and functional environment, dividing the room into individual areas, each of which requires the presence of a particular light.

In summary, the areas of the bathroom that require the presence of one or more light points are the following:

- the upper part of the walls and the ceiling;

- the area around the shower cubicle or tub;

- the wall that houses the sink and mirror;

- the floor or in any case the area below the line of the sink.

The most used lighting elements in a bathroom are:

- recessed ceiling or wall spotlights;

- applique with a contemporary or retro design;

- lights with adjustable intensity facing the ceiling;

- spotlights to be placed on the side of the mirror;

- hanging design lamps or chandeliers;

- indirect light wall lamps.

As for the colors, consider that the lights around the bathroom mirror must be a neutral white color so as not to alter the reflected images, while the other areas, especially the area surrounding the bathtub or shower, can be choose lamps in different colors, inspired by chromotherapy.

TIPS FOR A BATHROOM LIGHTING PROJECT

Before choosing the lights for your bathroom, carefully evaluate the style of the environment and, as we have seen, divide the room into some well-defined areas:

- the floor and the area below the sanitary ware and the sink;

- the upper part of the room and the ceiling;

- the walls at your eye level;

- the shower / tub and relaxation area;

- the mirror and sink area.

Also consider that in a modern and functional bathroom lighting project, it is important to equip each lamp with an independent switch and allow you to vary the intensity of the light emitted, so that everyone can customize the effect as desired. An important element is the lighting of the bathroom mirror, to be installed in a suitable position to give light to the face of the beholder without creating annoying reflections.

RECESSED LIGHTS FOR A SOFT ATMOSPHERE

If you want to reproduce the relaxing and enveloping atmosphere of a spa in your bathroom, you can choose LED lights in a warm color and place them behind a false ceiling or a plasterboard wall structure, in order to enhance the coverings and the architecture and convey a feeling of tranquility and relaxation.

Backlit mirror for a fantastic play of light

The lights installed on the back of the bathroom mirror allow you to create suggestive, simple and linear scenography's if the mirror has a regular shape or imaginative if you prefer mirrors with an original shape. The backlighting of the mirror generates an indirect, soft and suffused light, ideal as a piece of furniture even in a very large bathroom.

Applique on the mirror side for a vintage effect

If you want a bathroom with a retro atmosphere, choose two brass and colored glass appliques, with a vintage design, to be installed on the side of the mirror, with sanitary fittings, accessories and taps in the same style. An original alternative is to surround the rectangular bathroom mirror with a row of white light bulbs and opaque glass, to obtain a result similar to a theater dressing room.

Use mirrors to amplify the light

If your bathroom is small and with many shaded areas, perhaps because it has no windows, you can use the mirrors to enhance the effect of the lights, placing them across the wall and on two opposite sides of the room. Even the steel and glass accessories are suitable for illuminating a bathroom without natural light.

Furnish the bathroom with light effects

The lighting of a design bathroom requires light to become the protagonist of a furnishing project, creating new and original scenographies. You can choose lighting elements with a particular aesthetic, install the lamps so as to project the light on the walls to obtain shapes and designs or create plays of light and particular effects.

In a high-ceilinged bathroom, a series of small recessed spotlights, white or colored, convey the pleasant effect of a starry sky. Conversely, if you've lowered the bathroom with a false ceiling and have a floor to wall with one or two countertop sinks, you can light it up with a series of pendant lamps of different heights, using simple balloon bulbs.

To enhance a bathroom with a vintage style, with a freestanding bathtub and mirror with an important frame, choose a liberty chandelier in wrought iron and crystal, with a strong aesthetic impact, even better if in a bright color such as red or purple.

If, on the other hand, you want to embellish the atmosphere in a large bathroom, install linear lamps of different colors, to define each different area of the bathroom with a different chromatic effect. A very large bathroom also lends itself to being enriched with the creation of architectural elements, for example small niches with internal light or backlit columns.

SHOWER CUBICLE

A re we struggling with the construction of a new bathroom? Or are we simply replacing the tub with the shower? In both cases we will certainly find ourselves having to choose the shower box: how to find the solution that best suits our bathroom and our needs?

1. Choose the style that best suits your bathroom

Depending on the style that characterizes our bathroom, we can choose between different models of shower enclosures.

In general, there are 2 main types offered by the market:

- **SHOWER BOX WITH PROFILES** - suitable for bathrooms with a traditional taste, they can be equipped with acrylic or tempered glass panels. We can also find shower enclosures with steel-colored profiles, ideal to combine, for example, with a bathroom furnished with wooden furniture, rather than white, perfect for a classic total white bathroom.

- **SHOWER ENCLOSURE WITHOUT PROFILES** - ideal for environments in a minimalist design style, as we see in this elegant proposal, they are characterized exclusively by tempered glass panels, which can be transparent, printed, satin or silk-screened, depending on the effect we intend to create in our bathroom.

Tempered glass shower enclosures are generally less economical than those with acrylic panels, because the glass must be subjected to special treatments to meet the resistance and safety standards imposed by regulations. In case of breakage, the crystal plate shatters into a myriad of very small fragments, without points and not sharp, to minimize the danger.

2. Semicircular shower stalls

Distinguished by their characteristic curved shape and also called "quadrant", the semicircular shower enclosures are the ideal solution for showers positioned at an angle. In fact, they allow to save considerable space, making passage easier and at the same time offering an elegant and light structure.

On the market it is possible to find semicircular boxes with both hinged and sliding doors, even if generally the latter is the most used model, precisely for reasons of space.

WALK-IN SHOWER

The shower is a fundamental element of the home. Over time, due to the great importance it covers, the shower has undergone various evolutions in technique, use and design. The last of these is the walk- in shower, which completely revises the classic structure we are used to, re-proposing it in a minimal key.

Walk-in shower: a new shower concept

In the classic case, we are used to seeing a well-defined ceramic shower tray, with marked edges and a consistent height. On this, the closing glass plates or the sliding curtains are placed to ensure the closing of the shower box and to prevent the escape of water. It is significant to think of the fact that we are always used to talking about the shower enclosure, precisely because we imagine in our mind a space closed in on itself and different from the rest of the bathroom.

In walk-in showers, as the name suggests, we no longer have to open swing doors or curtains, enter and close them behind us.

The walk-in is in fact normally without at least one wall. That is to say that if we want to put it in a corner, then it is necessary to position a single glass plate in order to guarantee a single diaphragm but leaving one of the four sides open. From here you can guess the definition walk-in, that is a space in which you simply enter by walking.

We can even place the walk-in on one of the four sides of the bathroom, place a single glass in the center and leave two accesses free on the sides.

Under the banner of contemporary design, we will install a minimal glass, with essential lines and possibly without a frame.

Focusing now on the shower tray, which is also in line with the dematerialization process of the cabin and the glass, it is simplified, following a cleaner and simpler design. Even in some walk-in showers the ceramic plate no longer exists, but the space is obtained on the floor itself by making a cut in the tiles under which the water drain is placed.

ADVANTAGES AND DISADVANTAGES OF THE WALK-IN SHOWER

What are the advantages of walk-in showers and what are the disadvantages? Let's list them below to evaluate them thoroughly.

The advantages of walk-in showers:

The design is certainly more attractive and modern,

The space of the bathroom and the open shower are freed by being placed in direct communication with each other,

The cleaning of the shower is easier and more immediate, since the surfaces are minimal, without any setbacks, hinges, gaskets, stops.

The disadvantages of walk-in showers:

Since one of the four sides is missing, you will understand the problem of splashing water for yourself. This requires one of the two shower dimensions to be quite substantial, around 120cm or more.

Since the cabin no longer exists, you are in direct contact with the bathroom environment and therefore suffer more from the sensation of cold as the steam constantly escapes, while in the classic shower it accumulates keeping the box rather warm. In these cases, a heat source must be installed near the walk-in access.

Walk-in ideal size

From what has been explained so far, it is easy to understand that the dimensions of walk-in showers require more significant measures than closed solutions. Both to avoid splashes, and to avoid water leaks from below, and to guarantee the opening and fluid effect typical of this type of shower. For this reason, we advise against sizing the long side less than 120 cm, and the optimal is 150-160 cm or more.

What are the prices for walk-in showers?

Finally, what are the prices for the purchase of this type of shower?

Sometimes less than a normal shower. In fact, it is true that the box does not exist as we are used to normally understanding it. What remains is the plate, which, as we have seen, we cannot even install, and at least one perimeter glass plate. So, you can also spend 200 or 300 $ less than normal, but many other factors can make the difference! In fact, if you think about it, there are inexpensive ceramic shower trays from 110 $ and others in Corian that can cost several hundred $. Furthermore, if you want a great impact, you could choose quality brass or steel taps and the price could go up to 200 $ even for the components alone.

BATHROOM WITHOUT TILES

W hen it comes to bathroom cladding, the mind almost instinctively associates the solution of classic tiles.

Perhaps because this is what we have always seen, perhaps because the Italian tradition wants the covering in tiles, but from the post-war period to today this solution has always been followed.

In recent years, however, some alternatives to tiles have begun to be seen which, in my opinion, are capable of changing and improving the bathroom environment in several respects.

These finishes can in fact be:

- more functional,
- longer lasting,
- more hygienic,
- the most simple and quick to install.

But let's see them together ...

Resin bath

A resin bathroom is, of all, the preferred alternative to bathroom tiles.

It's like choosing a white kitchen, it's safe.

Often this solution is preferred due to its technical nature, as it is:

- very resistant to humidity (therefore less prone to mold growth),
- very hygienic because it is a waterproof material that is easy to clean,
- lasting over time as it hardly deteriorates,

- it can possibly be spread over the existing ceramics, speeding up and optimizing the renovations (before applying the resin layer, however, it is necessary to prepare a special primer that improves the adhesion of the resin itself and also avoids seeing the joints of the existing ceramics),
- it can be used both on the wall and on the floor without contraindications to its use inside the shower.

To these technical characteristics, however, it is necessary to add the aesthetic value that the use of resin allows.

Resin is in fact capable of creating an environment with a homogeneous finish and without joints and, by itself, of furnishing a bathroom making it elegant and timeless, allowing you to choose between different finishes, smooth or textured, and a wide range of colors, therefore not necessarily a gray bathroom.

Furthermore, the use of resin allows the possibility of completely covering washbasins, showers and bathtubs, adding value and uniqueness to the environment, as in modern rustic houses or inside a Turkish bath at home.

Microcement bathroom

Among the possible alternatives to a bathroom without tiles is the creation of a bathroom in microcement, a finish that has the same characteristics as resin.

Like resin, the use of microcement allows you to create a unique, homogeneous and joint-free environment, the customization of color and finishes, as well as the possibility of completely covering the other components of the bathroom furniture.

I know … you are wondering: but then how is microcement different from resin?

The answer lies in the nature of the microcement.

It is in fact a natural material, more breathable than resin (therefore the risk of mold is eliminated) and more resistant to wear.

But the real advantage of microcement is that, unlike some resins on the market that can tend to yellow, it is stable over time and does not undergo any color variation.

Enamel bath

The alternative of the enamel bathroom is instead a "comfortable" solution.

It is mainly used in renovations.

Enamel is a fairly easy-to-clean material that can be laid directly on existing tiles.

The use of enamel, however, maintains the reading of the joints, making the finish uniform: your bathroom will not be a real bathroom without tiles but it will certainly change its appearance.

Basically, it is like spreading a new covering color on top of the existing tiles, thus letting you see all that is in relief.

It has no real advantages over previous finishes.

On the contrary, the finish recreates a slightly grainy and glossy effect which, personally, I believe to be of medium-low quality.

Bathroom with wallpaper

One of the alternatives to tiles is the use of wallpaper; there are those who love it but personally I prefer to avoid using it in the bathroom.

Of course, it has several technical characteristics suitable for its use in the bathroom, such as excellent resistance to humidity, but I consider it an "easy" solution, which avoids the actual design of a modern bathroom.

Wallpaper works great in the commercial world, but indoors it should be used sparingly if the goal is to create a unique, elegant and comfortable home.

Bathroom covered in wood

Wood?

Yes, wood.

But doesn't wood swell with water?

It depends.

Pay attention.

Wood by its nature is a natural material that is highly affected by humidity.

Think about saunas.

The bathroom is perhaps the wettest room in the house, so the two don't really get along.

Excellent choice for an en-suite bathroom or a bathroom with a bathtub thanks to modern technologies that allow the creation and waterproofing of modern wood paneling, guaranteeing the treated material the same resistance to humidity as some of the materials mentioned above. It certainly needs more maintenance but the nature and warmth of the wood are unique.

To confirm this, I would like to point out that some of the best bathroom furniture manufacturers make their own wooden tubs and washbasins.

If they do it, those who study water and its characteristics on products from morning to night, why can't you have a wooden bathroom too?

We must eliminate the taboo of wood in the bathroom from the minds, as well as for the parquet in this environment.

Large format stoneware

But isn't stoneware a tile?

Yes, that's right ... But wait a minute ...

Stoneware is undoubtedly a ceramic tile; but if you are looking for an alternative to the tile because you want to avoid seeing the joints, the use of large-format stoneware slabs is a valid choice.

The large stoneware slabs allow you to recreate different finishes, from the uniform color (resin type) to that of marble or metals. With large-format slabs the joints are reduced to a minimum, thus making this solution an excellent alternative to the use of tiles.

A bathroom without tiles for me is a unique bathroom. Almost like a living room with a fireplace.

Certainly, these finishes help when you have to furnish an attic or build a house with a mezzanine, given the particularity of the sloping pitch at low heights.

I am strongly convinced that over time the tiles will disappear in favor of resin, microcement and wood.

Research in this sector is aiming at the transformation of traditional tiles into increasingly larger or smaller formats (mosaics and micromosaics) that make the bathroom in both cases as elegant as modern curtains.

The bathroom is in fact a very important room in the house, especially for those who want a modern home, and therefore it must be wonderful.

THINGS TO KNOW WHEN CHOOSING SANITARY WARE

O f all the bathroom elements, the sanitary fixtures seem to be the least important: if you believe that, it's only because you've always been lucky in your choices! If you make the wrong choices, in fact, you will understand that there is nothing worse than an uncomfortable and not very functional toilet. I have compiled the 6 things to consider before choosing the right components:

1. Choose a rimless toilet

We are used to seeing the toilet with that very thick inner ceramic edge from which the water comes out. It is ugly, uncomfortable and difficult to clean. For some years now the solution has existed:

rimless sanitary ware. More beautiful, quieter and easier to clean. There are only advantages to choosing this type of toilet.

2. Easy to clean toilet? No problem

Admit it, when you read "easy to clean" in the previous point, your eyes lit up. Well, get used to so many other comforts. First of all, because various manufacturers integrate titanium dioxide into the enamel layer, which naturally fights bacterial proliferation: no commitment is required on your part, your toilet will take care of not reproducing E. coli and many other bacteria! Even the extremely comfortable toilet seat is made for cleaning: many companies produce them to be easily removable, which means that you'll need to use the Allen wrench to remove the toilet seat from the toilet itself. Some companies produce a convenient button to press to be able to remove it, others even without any mechanism: simply pull upwards to release the toilet seat! Finally, cleaning will be very comfortable!

3. Ergonomic shapes of toilet to save water

In addition, up to 25% of the water we use during the day is used to rinse the toilet. For this reason, since 2014 the $pean Union has tried to encourage water saving in this sector by creating a water saving label. You know when you buy a new chandelier or a TV, which always has a label that perhaps shows the letter "A" to make you understand that it will consume little power? Toilets have the $pean Water Label, a label that shows in black and white how many liters the toilet needs for rinsing. At the time of the creation of the label the goal was to get to 3 liters and... guess what? We got there. Why this saving of liters is so important I can show you by making a quick calculation. Let's assume in an average family they use the toilet 20 times a day: we do the calculations with 3 possible different drains (9, 6 and 3 liters).

20 x 9 l = 180 liters / days x 365 = 65,700 liters / year

20 x 6 l = 120 liters / day x 365 = 43,800 liters / year

20 x 3 l = 60 liters / day x 365 = 21.900 liters / year

4. Raw materials and glazing

Choose a quality product. Of course, quality is more expensive but it guarantees better utility and better use

5. Choose a comfortable size

Hardly anyone has the giant bathrooms you see in magazines and photographs, we agree, so every inch recovered in the bathroom is worth gold. However, choosing sanitary ware with a small size becomes really uncomfortable and is therefore not recommended in all cases where it can be done without. The normal depth of the bathroom fixtures is usually 53 centimeters: the most "important" models even reach up to almost 60 centimeters. If you can, don't go below the standard. In fact, there are all the reduced sizes, which even reach up to 45 cm in depth, which allow you to save centimeters at the expense of comfort.

REPLACE THE TOILET BY YOURSELF

D o you need to replace the toilet in your home? Before turning to expensive plumbing, follow our advice! Do it yourself!

The toilet is a component that we cannot do without in our homes. For this reason, if major problems arise, it may need to be replaced. Your plumber will be happy to do this job for you, but in return you will pay dearly. So, if you prefer to save some cash, you can rely on DIY.

Replacing a toilet is not in fact too complicated an operation, even if it is important to carry out the work with the utmost attention and precision to avoid future recurring problems. Nowadays there are various models of this sanitary ware on the market, such as suspended ones. In this article, however, we show you how to change a classic floor-standing toilet. Here's how to do it!

TOILET MATERIAL

First you need to get everything you need. Needless to say, the first thing you need is a new toilet. Be careful which one you choose though. The new one must be of the same type and, if possible, of the same model as the one to be replaced. The reason for this is related to the connections with the various pipes, which may not coincide with the housing of the new toilet. As a matter of hygiene, it is preferable to carry out this work wearing gloves. To remove the old silicone, you will need a cutter. You will then need an eccentric gasket, to be inserted on the ceramic toilet drain, and a rubber gasket for the entrance to the cistern drain pipe.

In case the fixing holes of the new toilet do not coincide with the old one, (you can make sure with a measure) you will need a pair

Remodeling with an Architect

of pliers to remove the old plugs. In this case you will need new ones, as well as a drill with a suitable tip to drill the holes necessary to house them on the floor. Denatured alcohol can help you to better clean the floor, in order to prepare it for the next installation of the toilet.

To complete the job, you will need some silicone, to avoid any leaks, a spirit level, to ensure that the toilet is perfectly level, and a wrench of the right size to tighten the nuts.

How to do it

First of all, it is important to remember to close the water valve. Then start disassembling the old toilet, starting with the toilet seat. To extract the toilet from the floor, remove the fixing screws and remove the silicone at the base with the cutter. At this point you have to remove the toilet from the ground with light lateral movements until it rises. Then carefully remove it from the cistern exhaust pipe and the exhaust sling. The old toilet is now detached and you can start fitting the new one.

Evaluate the various distances. In particular, you will need to measure the distance between the plugs and the correspondence between the rear hole of the toilet and the drain pipe. If these coincide with those of the old one, you can continue with the installation phase by applying silicone on the base of the toilet. Conversely, we refer you to the following paragraphs to solve the problem.

You then insert the eccentric seal, shortening it with the cutter in the case where, as expected, it is longer than necessary. At this point, once the connections have been made, it is necessary to fix the toilet to the floor once and for all. So, make sure it is level, using any plastic wedges to even it out. Then tighten the nuts until the toilet is perfectly stable. Finally, also tighten the rubber gasket well and reassemble the seat.

Now there is nothing left to do but test the success of the replacement. Now reopen the water valve and once the cistern is full, flush the toilet. If you don't notice any leaks, the job will be done. If not, apply a little more silicone in the places where you notice any leaks.

Safety

Although it is not essential, before starting the replacement operation it is preferable to empty the toilet siphon. You can therefore use a liquid vacuum cleaner or soak old rags. Even if you decide not to proceed with this operation, it is still important that you flush the toilet several times, so that the water present is at least clean. In any case it is advisable to flush the toilet after closing the water valve, as the cistern will remain empty during the disassembly operations.

Practical advice

If you do not have a second bathroom, it is important to carefully evaluate the timing of the replacement work. Conversely, you would find yourself forced to use the neighbors' bathroom. However, there is no indicative time on which to base it, but this will depend on your skills and knowledge. For safety, however, it is better to estimate a longer time than what might actually be necessary.

If the distance between the plugs between the two toilets does not coincide, it is advisable to remove the old ones with a pair of pliers. To insert the new ones, place the toilet in its final position and, with a permanent marker, mark on the floor the exact point where to drill. Then remove the toilet and drill holes perpendicular to the floor at the established points. At this point, clean the holes of dust and clean the floor with denatured alcohol. In this way the silicone will have more grip. The latter must be applied to the lower part of the toilet in contact with the floor. Then you will have to arrange the toilet in the right position. However, if the work involves particular situations, especially if the replacement of the toilet concerns old houses, it is possible to apply the silicone only after the toilet is completely fixed.

If, on the other hand, the rear hole does not coincide with the drain pipe of the toilet cistern, it is preferable to purchase a new cistern with external pipe.

HOW TO REPLACE A SINK YOURSELF

BATHROOM
Remodeling with an Architect

Bathroom sinks can get chipped, scratched, or stained, and you may want to change one to give your bathroom a newer, tidier look. Replacing a sink can be time consuming but it shouldn't be difficult to do, and it will definitely make the whole room look more beautiful.

STEPS

1

With a tape measure, measure the old sink. When you install a new one, it will have to fit in the old plan. Note the length, depth and width of both the sink and the surface on which you will mount it.

2

Buy a new sink. Bring the measurements of the old sink and counter with you, to make sure you choose one of the right sizes.

3

Remove the water. The knob to turn off the water is usually located under the sink, and to make sure the water has turned off, try turning the knob on the faucet.

4

Place a bucket under the siphon. The first thing to do is to remove the exhaust pipes.

Using parrot pliers, loosen the siphon bolts.

Place the siphon on the bucket, after gently removing it from the sink.

5

Unhook the hot and cold-water pipes from the faucet with a wrench. Assembling a sink involves having to spend time under it to remove various pieces.

6

With a screwdriver, remove the screws holding the sink to the counter.

7

With a utility knife, remove all silicone residues between the countertop and the sink.

8

Lift the old sink off the counter. The surface must be clean and flat, so eliminate all silicone residues.

9

Remove the faucet and drain pipes from the old sink if you want to reuse them with the new one as well.

10

Fit the old sink and drain to the new sink. You need to seal the pieces well, so apply a layer of silicone to the faucet and base of the drain. If you buy a new tap, consult the instruction manual for installation.

11

Apply silicone to the bottom edge of the sink. Place it along the space provided on the top, fix it in place and remove excess silicone with wipes.

12

Connect the sink to the countertop with screws, applying them from the countertop towards the sink. Make sure it is securely attached.

13

Re-connect the water pipes with the wrench and the siphon with the parrot pliers. Do not over-tighten the screws.

Put the water valves back on. Leave the bucket under the sink while you test the pieces, in case there are any leaks.

Open the hot water valve and then the cold-water valve. If there are any leaks, turn off the water and put the gaskets back on, also using Teflon tape on the pipe.

Here is your new sink, installed quickly and easily. Your new sink is not only practical and functional, it also gives that extra touch to your bathroom.

ESSENTIAL BATHROOM ACCESSORIES

They are called accessories, but they are fundamental elements of bathroom furniture.

They not only complete the aesthetics of an environment, but make it practical and functional.

The latest trends offer bathroom accessories with minimal lines, often compact and multi-purpose.

Sometimes they are part of the sanitary ware collections, but the beauty is to feel free to mix, experiment with new combinations and take advantage of the versatility of each object.

But how to choose bathroom accessories? Some useful tips to avoid making mistakes.

SPACE.

The element to be evaluated at the outset, not only because "taking measurements" is a must, but also because the bathroom is one of the most used rooms and the space must necessarily be optimized.

In larger rooms, accessories are used to furnish, to make them even more welcoming and pleasant.

To be considered together with the space there is functionality.

As obvious as it is that bathroom accessories must be functional, it cannot be taken for granted that they actually are. In fact, various factors come into play, such as the materials, the shapes, the installation.

The perfect bathroom accessories fulfill their function and multiply the possibilities of use.

Wall-mounted bathroom accessories are indispensable for small rooms because they allow you to take advantage of every surface... even the vertical ones.

Soap holders are also shelves and the shelves become towel holders!

The roll holders installed on the wall can also be used as magazine holders.

Larger rooms, used by the whole family, can be furnished with practical and versatile accessories.

Stools can also be used as magazine racks or towel racks (for those who want to keep the sponges in sight!).

More and more often the traditional "toilet brushes", in the free-standing version, also house the toilet roll holder or the towel holder.

Free-standing towel racks are real furnishing elements.

HYGIENE.

In the bathroom, hygiene is fundamental and in the choice of bathroom accessories it is better to get shapes and materials that allow you to sanitize easily, frequently and in depth, avoiding bad smells and the formation of unpleasant molds.

This mainly applies to toothbrush holders, soap holders and the toilet brush where water stagnation is created.

Shopping.

The budget factor is essential. The range of possibilities is now almost infinite because there are so many manufacturing companies.

But be careful because often evaluating only the cost of the objects you forget about all the other important factors.

Poor quality bathroom accessories can easily deteriorate in contact with water, but also favor the reproduction of molds.

STYLE.

You can indulge in this, there are no rules. "Neutral" style accessories are often preferred, perhaps in polished or brushed steel with traditional shapes, but more and more frequently it is preferred to completely break with the style and furnishings of the bathroom by choosing bright colors, innovative materials and shapes.

A separate chapter concerns mirrors, bathroom accessories essential for their function, but also for versatility.

The correct installation of mirrors allows you to make an environment optically larger and if combined with the right lighting they become indispensable elements.

With precision lights or backlights, the possibilities are different.

Then there are the container mirrors, allies of small spaces. To be evaluated in the presence of countertop washbasins on shelves, but also to multiply the usable space with a practically invisible solution.

When we think of a bathroom, not only the bathroom fixtures, the shower and the bathtub come to mind, but also all those accessories that make the room welcoming, practical and functional to be lived in everyday life. Of course, we are talking about bathroom accessories, essential to complete the furniture and to guarantee you all the comforts you need. In this article we find out what are the essential bathroom accessories and some tips for choosing them.

5 ESSENTIAL BATHROOM ACCESSORIES

Before discovering which are the objects for the bathroom that just cannot be missing and which we could never do without, let's make a clarification. An important thing is to keep them coordinated as much as possible, in order to obtain a tidy and harmonious overall effect. The same must be done with the style of the bathroom: if you have chosen contemporary bathroom fixtures and furniture, the accessories must also have that style and the same must be done for the colors. In short, try to coordinate everything as best as possible.

Towel holder

Could you imagine a bathroom without a stand to hang towels from? The towel rail is essential for convenience in the bathroom. The most practical and less bulky are those that hang on the wall: they can have the shape of a ring or a longer or shorter bar, equipped with a movable or fixed arm. Likewise, provide a robe hook near the shower exit.

Soap holder

The soap dish is very visible so it is important that it is chosen with care. You can choose it in the saucer version if you prefer to use a bar of soap or in the dispenser version if you prefer liquid soap. We find them in many different materials, but the most common are ceramic and, increasingly, plastic. If you are looking for something more particular you can opt for wood or stone.

Toothbrush holder

Next to the soap dish, on the sink or in any case nearby, we always find the toothbrush holder. These two-bathroom accessories must be perfectly coordinated because they are close together: they do not necessarily have to be identical but the style, material and colors must still be in harmony because the eye will always see them at the same time.

Bathroom floor lamp

A widely used solution is that of the bathroom floor lamp which allows you to purchase a single object for different purposes: in particular, the floor lamps consisting of toilet roll holder and toilet brush holder, two other essential bathroom accessories, are very popular. You can also buy them separately and attach the roll holder to the wall, but the floor lamp is certainly a simpler and more practical solution.

Waste bin

Finally, among the objects for the bathroom it is perhaps the most useful element in everyday life: we are talking about the waste bin. Having a small basket at hand where you can throw away what you don't need while in the bathroom is essential so don't forget to buy one that is coordinated with all the other bathroom accessories. It is usually placed near the sink for greater convenience.